Gentlemen's Garment Cutting

- Trousers, Vests, Coats, Overgarments, Corpulent Figures, and Variations -

By

Percival Thickett

Copyright © 2011 Read Books Ltd.
This book is copyright and may not be
reproduced or copied in any way without
the express permission of the publisher in writing

British Library Cataloguing-in-Publication Data
A catalogue record for this book is available from
the British Library

Dressmaking and Tailoring

Dressmaking and Tailoring broadly refers to those who make, repair or alter clothing for a profession. A dressmaker will traditionally make custom clothing for women, ranging from dresses and blouses to full evening gowns (also historically called a mantua-maker or a modiste). Whereas a tailor will do the same, but usually for men's clothing - especially suits. The terms essentially refer to a specific set of hand and machine sewing skills, as well as pressing techniques that are unique to the construction of traditional clothing. This is separate to 'made to measure', which uses a set of pre-existing patterns. Usually, a bespoke tailored suit or dress will be completely original and unique to the customer, and hence such items have been highly desirable since the trade first appeared in the thirteenth century. The Oxford English Dictionary states that the word 'tailor' first came into usage around the 1290s, and undoubtedly by this point, tailoring guilds, as well as those of cloth merchants and weavers were well established across Europe.

As the tailoring profession has evolved, so too have the methods of tailoring. There are a number of distinctive business models which modern tailors may practice, such as 'local tailoring' where the tailor is met locally, and the garment is produced locally too, 'distance tailoring', where a garment is ordered from an out-of-town tailor, enabling cheaper labour to be used -

which, in practice can now be done on a global scale via e-commerce websites, and a 'travelling tailor', where the man or woman will travel between cities, usually stationing in a luxury hotel to provide the client the same tailoring services they would provide in their local store. These processes are the same for both women's and men's garment making.

Pattern making is a very important part of this profession; the construction of a paper or cardboard template from which the parts of a garment are traced onto fabric before cutting our and assembling. A custom dressmaker (or tailor) frequently employs one of three pattern creation methods; a 'flat-pattern method' which begins with the creation of a sloper or block (a basic pattern for a garment, made to the wearer's measurements), which can then be used to create patterns for many styles of garments, with varying necklines, sleeves, dart placements and so on. Although it is also used for womenswear, the 'drafting method' is more commonly employed in menswear and involves drafting a pattern directly onto pattern paper using a variety of straightedges and curves. Since menswear rarely involves draping, pattern-making is the primary preparation for creating a cut-and-sew woven garment. The third method, the 'pattern draping method' is used when the patternmaker's skill is not matched with the difficulty of the design. It involves creating a muslin mock-up pattern, by pinning fabric directly on a dress form, then transferring the muslin outline and markings onto a paper pattern or using the muslin as the pattern itself.

Dressmaking and tailoring has become a very well respected profession; dressmakers such as Pierre Balmain, Christian Dior, Cristóbal Balenciaga and Coco Chanel have gone on to achieve international acclaim and fashion notoriety. Balmain, known for sophistication and elegance, once said that 'dressmaking is the architecture of movement.' Whilst tailors, due to the nature of their profession - catering to men's fashions, have not garnered such levels of individual fame, areas such as 'Savile Row' in the United Kingdom are today seen as the heart of the trade.

GENTLEMEN'S GARMENT CUTTING

By PERCIVAL THICKETT

(*Author of " Defects and Remedies," " Body Coats," etc.*)

TROUSER CUTTING

NORMAL DRAFT. Diagram 1

FEATURES :—*Medium width at knee and bottom. Plain bottoms.*
MEASURES :—*30" waist; 36" seat; 41" side seam; 29" inside leg; 20" knee width; 16" bottom.*

INSTRUCTIONS FOR DRAFTING

FOR drafting purposes and to make the working out of the fractional quantities a little less formidable, the seat and waist measures are halved as follows :—Seat 18" ; waist 15". Line 0–0 in section A of the diagram can either represent the primal construction line when making a pattern or the selvedge when drafting straight on to the cloth.

If there is no distinct stripe in the material, and it is necessary to be strictly economical, point 18 section A may be brought nearer to the selvedge when the pattern is being marked round.

¼" seams are provided through the draft.

THE TOPSIDES. SECTION A

Draw the construction line 0–0 ;
1 from 0 = the inside leg length (29") ;
2 from 0 = the side seam|length (41"), plus making up allowance, say ¼" ;
Square out from the above points.
3 from 1 = one-third seat (6") ;
4 from 3 = one-sixth seat (3") ;
5 from 4 = one-sixth seat plus ¼" (3¼") ;
Square down from point 3 and up from point 4.
6 is located where the line from 3 intersects the base line from 0 ;
7 is located where the line from 4 intersects the line from 2.
8 from 7 = 2" : square out ;
9 from 8 = half waist plus ¼" for two seams ;
10 is obtained by springing out ¼" from 9 ;
Strike a line midway across the angle at fork outlined by points 5, 4, and 7 ;
11 from 4 = half 4 to 5 plus ¼" ;
Shape the fork curve from 12, which is one-sixth seat up from 4 ;
13 from 4 = one-sixth seat (3") ;

TROUSER CUTTING

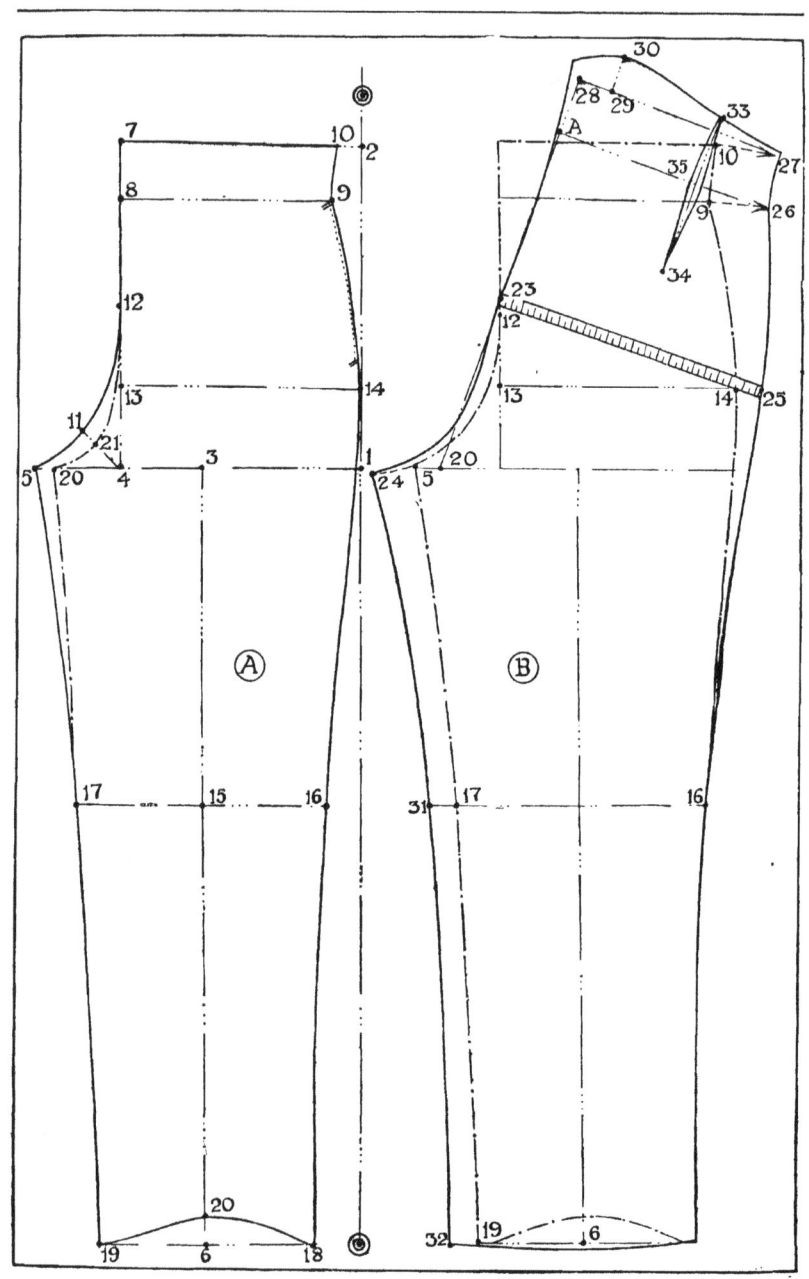

DIAGRAM 1.

TROUSER CUTTING

14 is located by squaring out from 13;
15 from 3 = half leg length less 2" (12½) for knee line; 16 from 15 = one-fourth knee (5");
17 from 15 is the same.
18 from 6 = one-fourth bottom (4");
19 from 6 in the same.
Having joined 9 and 10, continue down through 14 to 16 and 18 (ignoring point 1);
From 5 curve to 17 and continue to 19;
20 from 6 in this instance is ¾", but the quantity will vary with the type of bottom required.
For instance, if the bottom is required wider than the measure given, then this distance can be decreased to allow the fronts to fall more on to the boot. The reverse would apply in the case of a narrower bottom.

Dress

This is a sartorial term used in defining the quantity by which one side of the fork is reduced to accommodate the requirements of the figure.
A man usually "dresses" on the left side—this is readily ascertained at the time of measuring—we therefore reduce the right topside fork as follows:
20 from 5 = ¾";
21 from 11 is also ¾";
Curve from 12 through 21 to 20 and down towards 17.

The Undersides. Section B

In preparation for the drafting of the undersides it is necessary, of course, to cut out the constructed topside.
Having laid this in a convenient position proceed as follows:
23 from 12 = ¼";
Draw the seat line from 20 through 23 and forward towards 28;
Using 17 as a pivot, sweep out from 5 to 24;
24 from 5 = 1½";
25 from 23 = the seat measure plus 2" (20) less the distance across the topsides from 13 to 14. The 2" addition represents the allowance for seams and ease.
Using 16 as a pivot, sweep from 9 and 10 as shown;
Fix point A (on the seat line) ¼" above the topside;
26 from A = half waist plus 1½" (9");
Spring out from 26 on to top sweep at 27.
Using the seat line 20 to A square from 28 to 27;
29 from 28 = 1½";
30 from 29 = 1½";
Shape the top as shown, springing out ½" at 28;
Hollow the fork ¼" inside the seat line from 23 to 24;
31 from 17 and 32 from 19 are each 1";
Curve the bottom of the underside ¼" below 6;
For the back dart or "fish" mark 2½" from 27 to 33;
Square down 6" from 33 to 34.
The deepest part of the dart lies at point 35 on the line A to 26, where ¼" is taken out.

Notes on the Draft

The crease in the finished trouser should come down the centre line 3 to 20.
When a more roomy seat is required to go with a wider knee and bottom, point 14 can be brought outside the construction line and the quantity added over the seat measure from 23 to 25 increased.
Although it is detrimental to the fit at the back, some cutters prefer to omit the dart at 33, thus reducing the cost of making. When this is required, the quantity from A to 26 should read: Half waist plus ¼".

TROUSER CUTTING

CORPULENT DRAFT. Diagram 2

FEATURES :—*Fly fronts. Plain bottoms. Side pockets. Moderate width at knee and bottom.*
MEASURES :—48" *waist ;* 45" *seat ;* 42" *side seam ;* 28" *inside leg ;* 23" *knee ;* 19" *bottom.*

DISPROPORTION

THROUGHOUT the Trade the accepted proportionate or ideal waist is determined by deducting 6" from the measured seat. Therefore where a comparison of the seat and waist shows a difference of more or less than this standardised quantity, the figure is said to be disproportionate. For the purposes of this draft we will further add that as the difference becomes gradually less, so is the figure progressing towards the corpulent state. Opinions vary respecting the stage at which a man becomes corpulent, but this need not worry the student, as the system laid down automatically adjusts the draft to meet all degrees of disproportion.

FORMULA

In order to allocate correctly the waist increment in the draft, it is necessary to know the correct amount of disproportion. This is found as follows :—Seat 45" less 6" gives the proportionate waist 39". Compare the measured waist (48") with this and we have the amount of disproportion, viz. 9".

INSTRUCTIONS FOR DRAFTING

All points below the fork line (1) are found as in the previous draft.

To accommodate the straightness of the back waist and the erectness of carriage, which is typical of such a figure, a little variation is made to run of the seat line 20 and 22.

In measuring up the waist of the undersides there is no necessity for the 1" allowance for the back fish or dart, as this is omitted for figures of such proportions.

The half-seat 22½" and half-waist 24" are the quantities referred to in the instructions below.

TROUSER CUTTING

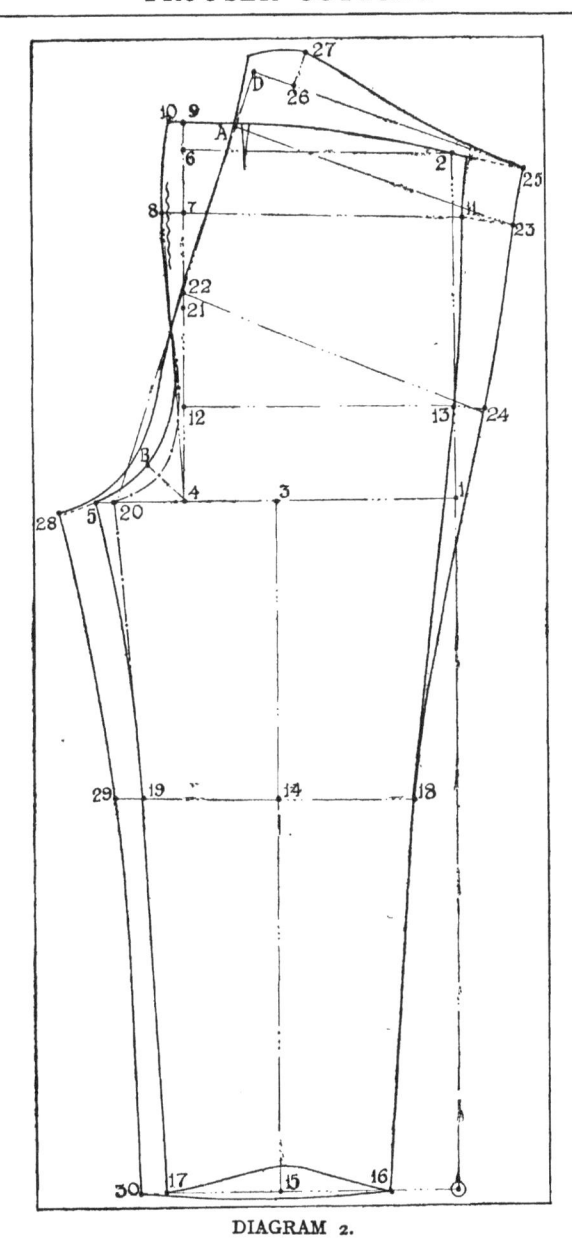

DIAGRAM 2.

TROUSER CUTTING

The Topsides

Square lines from o ;
1 from o = the leg length 28″ ;
2 from o = the side length 42″ plus allowance for making-up ;
Square out from these points.
3 from 1 = one-third seat (7¼″) ;
4 from 3 = one-sixth seat (3¾″) ;
5 from 4 = one-sixth seat ; no addition is made as in the previous draft.
Square down from 3 and up from 4 ;
6 is located where line from 4 intersects the line from 2 ;
7 from 6 = 2½″ ;
8 from 7 = one-eighth disproportion (1¼″) ;
9 from 6 = 7 to 8 ;
10 from 9 is ¼″ less than 7 to 8 ;
11 from 8 = half waist plus ½″ ;
12 from 4 = one-sixth seat (3¾″) ;
13 is found by squaring across from 12 ;
14 is half leg less 2″ from 3 for knee-line ;
Square out on either side of 14 ;
16 from 15 = one-fourth bottom 4¾″ ;
17 from 15 is the same ;
18 from 14 = one-fourth knee 5¼″ ;
19 from 14 is the same.
To complete the topsides, draw from 11 through 13, straight down to 18 and 16.
B from 4 = half 4 to 5 plus ¼″ ;
Join 8 to 4 and use this line as a guide when shaping fork.
20 for the dress side is ¾″ from 5 ;
Mark in the same quantity at B and follow the run of dot and dash line.
Hollow bottom ¼″ above 15.

The Undersides

21 from 4 = one-third seat plus ½″ ;
22 from 21 = ½″ ;
Draw through 22 from 20 and continue up towards D ;
Using point 18 as a pivot, sweep 11 and 13 ;
23 from A = half waist plus ¼″ ;
24 from 22 is the seat measure plus 2″ (24½) less 12 to 13 ;
Shape the side seam from 23 through 24 to knee and spring out to 25 on top line.
Square D–25 by line 20–22 ;
26 is 2″ from D and 27 is 1½″ above 26 ;
28 is 1½″ from 5 ;
29 and 30 are each 1″ from the topsides.

Notes on the Draft

In order to distribute the round more evenly over the front, a small dart is taken out in the topside (near A). This dart is also influential in keeping the top edge nice and snug to the figure.
The quantity from 21 to 22 must vary with the degree of disproportion as follows :—Where the amount recorded is 6″, 21 to 22 should read ¼″, and in extreme cases, such as a 12″ disproportion, this distance should be made ¾″, and so on.
Some fat men stand and walk with their feet well apart. This should be carefully noted at the time of measuring, and draft adjusted by moving line 3–15 (½″ to 1″) nearer the side line 1–0. Normal cut trousers on such figures would swing away from the inner side of boot.

TROUSER CUTTING

STYLE DETAILS AND TOP FINISHES

DIAGRAM 3 has been devoted to a display of various styles of finish that the trouser cutter may be called upon to produce. No apology is offered for the inclusion of such back-dated top finishes as Whole Falls, French Bearers, etc. These are still being asked for in some of the Provincial trades, and there are many cutters whose careers do not date back to the period when such styles were in universal use.

PLEATED TOPS. SECTION A

This is a modern top finish, introduced to distribute the extra hip size that present fashion demands.

The pleats are inserted in the top side, the allowance being made at side-seam. In some instances one pleat only is introduced, but the allowance made is the same as for the two.

1 is the waist-line, 1½″ below the ordinary top or 1½″ less than the body-rise from 0.

2 from 1 = half waist plus ½″;

3 from 2 = 2″ for the pleats;

5 from 4 = one-third 2 to 3;

When measuring up the seat to point 6, add 2½″ to 3″ over the measure.

7 for the first pleat is situated on the centre line;

8 is midway between 8 and 3;

10 is half waist plus 1½″ as usual, but the top is kept straight and the vee is made without the convex curve.

TOP BAND

This is cut 2″ wide and the length from 11 to 12 = half waist plus ½″.

The dash line extension shows the addition necessary when the right side is required to go across the fly.

Curve the band ¼″ below 12.

SIDE POCKET. SECTION B

The opening for this commences at the waist at (1) and extends 6″ to 6¼″ down the side seam of topside to 2. The facing shown at 3 may be left grown-on or cut separately. The outline of the pockets is shown by dash lines.

FLY AND FRENCH BEARER. SECTION B

Both the right and left fly are cut together, the left or dress side being used for the shaping as shown at 4. The width is about 2½″.

French Bearers are adjuncts frequently ordered by stout men. The bearer, which is lined and interlined, is an extension of the button fly (see 5) and carries the two holes for fastening. These fasten on to a short strap inserted in the left side seam and shown at 6.

P.T.U.'S. SECTION C

This particular bottom finish requires a shorter leg length than the ordinary plain style, the amount being ¾″ to 1″ according to the width of bottom.

1 to 2 is the actual length required.

1 to 7 and 7 to 5 represent the width of turnings.

3 and 4 represent the position of the top of the turn-up.

Square down from 3 and 4 to locate 5 and 6;

From 1 and 2 shape to 7 and 8 going ⅛″ outside the line from 4.

Add ½″ to ¾″ below 5 to 6 for turning.

WHOLE OR FULL FALLS. SECTION D

In this finish flys are dispensed with, the front seam being sewn up.

As in the case of pleated top, the part above the waist line is cut away, as shown at 1 and 2. A bearer is then cut to make up the deficiency, as shown by dotted lines at 3 and 4.

TROUSER CUTTING

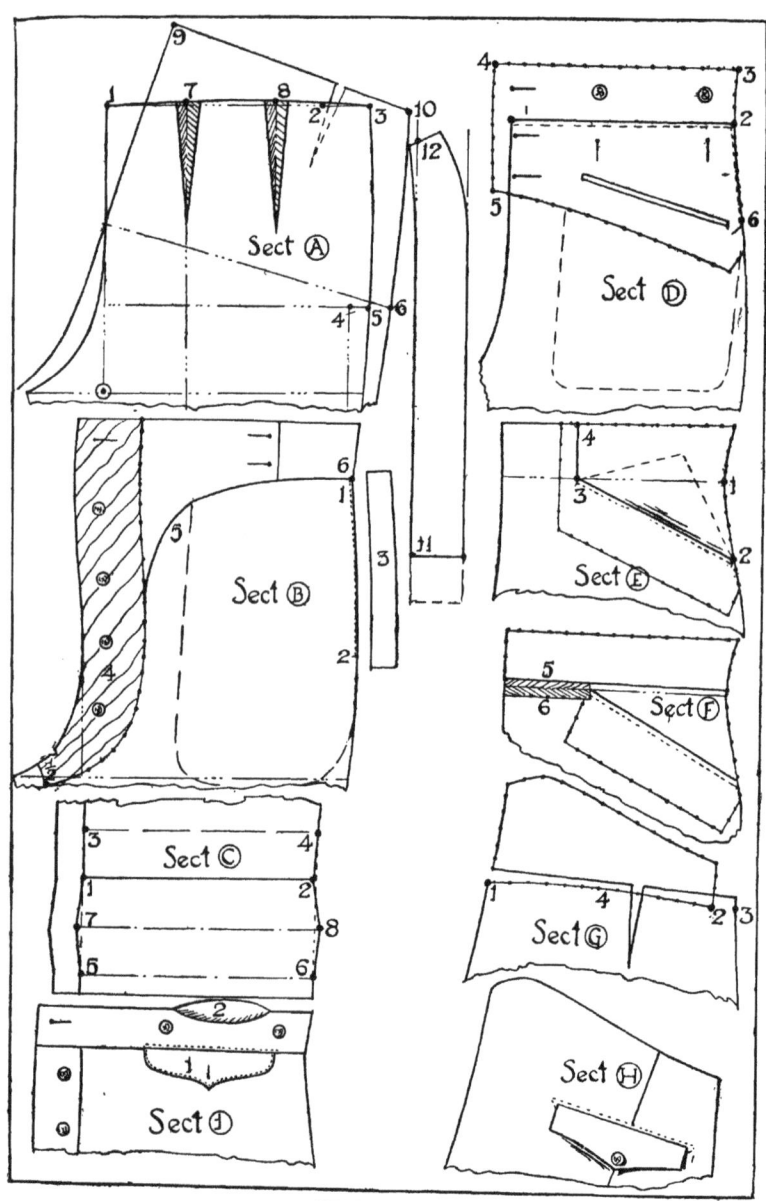

DIAGRAM 3.

TROUSER CUTTING

The front of the bearer projects $\frac{1}{2}"$ beyond the front and is made 4" deep.

6 is $3\frac{1}{2}"$ down from 2 for the slit at the side, the bearer extending below this.

Jetted pockets are placed in the bearer, $\frac{1}{4}"$ from the tack at 6, and extending 6" in an upward incline.

The bearer, 3 to 6, is sewn to the undersides.

The topsides, 1 to 2, are faced deeply and have holes inserted to fasten to corresponding buttons on the bearer.

Dress can be taken out in the usual way, but in heavy materials both sides are left the same.

Cross Pockets. Sections E and F

For this particular finish the back tack is placed at $3\frac{1}{4}"$ down from the waist (1 to 2); 3 from 2 (on waist line) is 6";

The tops are slit down from 4 to 3 and the right-hand portion is cut away to form the facing, as illustrated by dash lines.

The bearer (dotted line) is then cut to fill in the vacancy, $\frac{1}{4}"$ being allowed beyond points 3 and 4 for seams.

Section F demonstrates how the bearer would be cut where there is a top welt.

The topsides in this case are cut away a seam's width above the waist line (5).

The bearer is shown in dotted lines, a seam being allowed below the waist at 6.

Seat Piece. Section G

Where short lengths or "long" customers are the rule, it may be necessary to piece out the undersides. The dotted lines here illustrate how this should be carried out, when there is a dart in the waist.

1 and 2 are $\frac{1}{4}"$ down from the body part for seam allowance.

2 from 3 = 1" the amount taken up by the dart.

Shape from 1 to 2, hollowing a little at 4 to give spring to the tops.

Hip Pocket. Section H

The position of the hip or "pistol" pocket is situated 1" from the side-seam at 1 and 3" to $3\frac{1}{2}"$ from the top at the fore end. The flap, which covers the mouth, is 5" wide, and the back end $4\frac{1}{2}"$ from the top.

Cash and Fob Pocket. Section I

The cash pocket (1) is 5" long and is placed on the waist line with the rear end 1" out from the side seam.

The fob pocket (2) is placed between the two front buttons, the tops being hollowed out and a deep facing sewn on to the rear of the pocket to fill in the vacancy and to give easy access.

PLATE II

GEORGE DUNCAN, WEARING HIS SPECIALLY SELECTED DESIGN IN "SPORTEX."
By courtesy of Dormeuil Frères.

PLUS FOURS
Diagram 4

FEATURES :—*The modern style of this garment is represented with a medium " fall over " and moderate width in the legs ; pleated tops and waistband ; strap and buckle at the small for fastening.*
MEASURES :—32" *waist ;* 38" *seat ;* 42" *side ;* 30" *leg ;* 12" *round small of leg ;* 13" *round calf.*

The leg and side measures are taken in exactly the same fashion as for trousers.

INSTRUCTIONS FOR DRAFTING

THE full side measure not being used, we have dispensed with the side line in this draft.

The process of producing the pattern is the same as in previous drafts, the topside being cut out and the underhalf drafted by it.

There is a decided change in the run of the seat line in this draft from what was shown for trousers. It has a much straighter or upright run and is well hollowed in the fork. This change has been introduced to give a clean hanging underhalf below the brow of the seat.

The half-seat (19") and waist (16") measures are referred to in the details below.

THE DRAFT. SECTION A
Draw a line from o.
1 from o = one-third seat (6¾") ;
2 from 1 = one-sixth seat plus ¼" (3¾") ;
3 from 2 = one-sixth seat less ¼" (2⅝") ;
Square up from 2 to 4.
The difference between the leg and side measures is 12".
4 from 2 = the above difference less 1½" (10½").
Square out from 4.
5 from 2 = half 2 to 3 plus ¼" ;
6 from 2 = ¼ seat ;
Square out to locate point 7.
8 from 7 = 1¼", but this quantity can be varied to accord with the amount of bagginess required.
9 from 4 = half waist plus ½" for seams and 2" for pleats (10¼") ;

Give a little round from 4 to 9.
10 from 1 = half leg length ;
Square out on either side.
11 from 10 = 7¾" for a medium " fall over."
12 from 11 = one-fourth small measure plus 1" for gathering or pleats.
13 from 11 = 11 to 12 ;
14 from 10 = 1½" more than 11 to 13 ;
15 from 10 = 2½" more than 11 to 12 ;
Both the above quantities can be varied for style purposes.
16 from 12 = ½" ;
Shape side and leg seams as shown in diagram.
The first pleat is situated on the centre line and the rear one midway between the side seam and the front pleat.
Join 16 and 13 dropping ¼" for seam and giving a little round.

PLUS FOURS

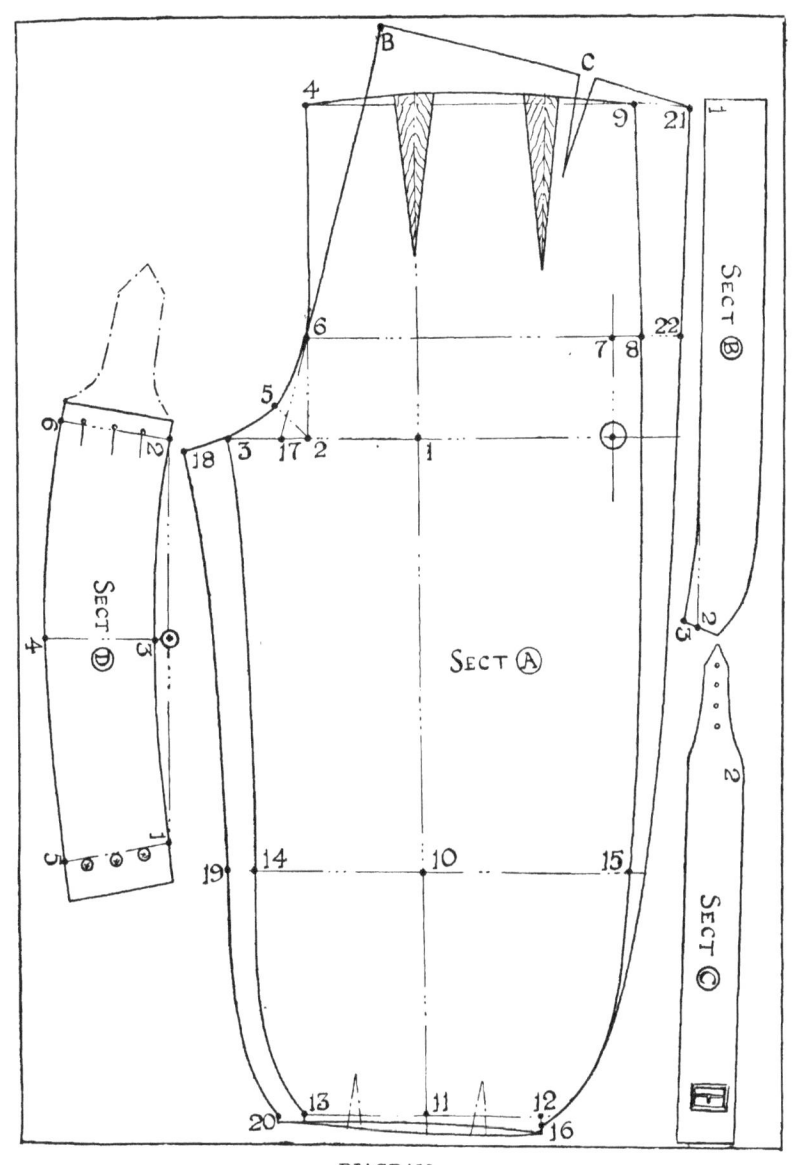

DIAGRAM 4.

PLUS FOURS

UNDERSIDE

17 from 3 = half the distance 3 to 2 plus ⅜";
Draw through 6 from 17 for seat line;
18 from 3 = 1½";
Curve run from 6 as shown.
19 from 14 = 1";
20 from 13 = 1";
Shape leg seam through 19 from 18.
21 from seat line in region of B = half waist plus 1½".
B is definitely located by squaring from the seat line (17–6) to 21.
Take ½" vee out at C as shown.
22 from 8 = 1¼";
Shape side seam from 21 through 22 and down to 16.

TOP BAND. SECTION B

The width of the band is 2".
2 from 1 = the waist measure 16" plus ¼" for seam.
3 from 2 = ½";
Shape from 1 curving down to 3.

STRAP. SECTION C

This is the strap that is sewn round the base of the legs of the knickers. It carries eyelet holes which connect with a buckle sewn about 1¼" from the opposite end. This is the most popular method of finishing the bottoms.
The width is about 2" with seams and the length from 1 to 2 equals the size of the small. The extension for fastening end is about 3" in length.

AN ALTERNATIVE FINISH. SECTION D

The broad band is a relic of the cycling knickerbocker days, but it is still asked for by quite a number of people.
1 from 0 = half small plus ¼";
2 from 0 is the same.
3 from 0 = half the difference between the calf and small measures (½).
4 from 3 = 3½";
Curve the base parallel with the top.
5 and 6 are each half the calf measure plus ¼", from 4.
Add 1¼" for button stand at 1 to 5 and ½" for the hole side at 2 and 6.
Three buttons and holes comprise the fastening as a rule, but some favour an extension (similar to that given on the narrow strap) for fastening to a buckle in place of the buttons and holes.

NOTES ON THE DRAFT

For corpulent figures the disproportion will be applied in the same manner as for trousers, point 4 being advanced and the tops raised above the squared line.
Pleats are not recommended, however, for such figures.
Darts or pleats can be utilised as a means of bringing the bottoms to fit in the strap. An alternative method is to gather or draw-in the bottom with a thread.
Where a distinct check is embodied in the design of the material, care will have to be exercised when laying the pattern out on the material.

RIDING BREECHES

Diagram 5

FEATURES :—*Fly front ; moderate side pouch ; centre front knee fastening ; cross pockets.*

MEASURES :—32″ *waist ;* 38″ *seat ;* 14″ *length to knee ;* 16½″ *length to small or hollow ;* 19½″ *length to calf ;* 13½″ *knee width ;* 12″ *small width ;* 13½″ *calf width ; inside leg length* 32″ *; outside leg* 44″.

INSTRUCTIONS FOR DRAFTING

COMPARED with ordinary trousers riding breeches require a little different treatment in the trunk section of the draft, to provide the necessary ease for mounting and for the astride position when in the saddle.

The position of the fastening on the leg is affected by the situation of line E in the topsides. If the fastening is required more to the side of the leg, the distance 12 to E must be increased.

Half seat (19″) and half waist (32″) are the measures referred to in the instructions below.

THE DRAFT

Draw lines from 0.
1 from 0 = one-third of seat (6⅜) ;
2 from 1 = one-sixth of seat (3⅛) ;
3 from 2 = one-sixth of seat plus ¾″ ;
Square up from 2.
4 from 2 = the body rise (12″) found by deducting the inside leg 32 from the outside 44 ;
Add making-up allowance, say ½″ ;
5 from 4 = 2″ ;
6 from 5 = half waist plus ½″ ;
7 is located by springing out to top-line from 6.
8 from 2 = half the distance 2 to 3 plus ¼″ ;
9 from 2 = one-third seat (6⅜) minus ½″ ;
Shape fork curve as shown.
10 from 1 = ¾″ ;
Square down ;
11 from 10 = 1½″ for ease ;
12 from 11 = length to knee 14″ ;
13 from 11 = length to small 16½″ ;
14 from 11 = length to calf 19½″ ;
The average distances of 2½″ from 12 to 13 and 3″ from 13 to 14 can be used where the inside trouser leg is the only length measure available.
A from 12 = ¼ knee width 3⅜ ;
B and C are located by squaring down from A ;
15 from A = half knee (6¾″) ;
16 from B = half small (6″) ;
17 from C = half calf (6¾″) ;
Shape inseam through 15, 16 and 17, commencing at 3 ;
E is ½″ out from 12 ;
Square down to H ;
18 from 0 = 1½″ ;
Join to E ;
19 is midway between 18 and E ;
20 from 19 = 2½″ to 3″ ;
Shape side seam from 18 to 7 and down from 18 to E ;
Drop the fronts ¾″ at 4.

UNDERSIDE

21 from 3 = ¾″ ;
Draw from 21 through 9 for seat line ;
22 from 3 = 1½″ ;
Sweep out from 3 pivoting at 15 ;
Square 23 to 24 by seat line.

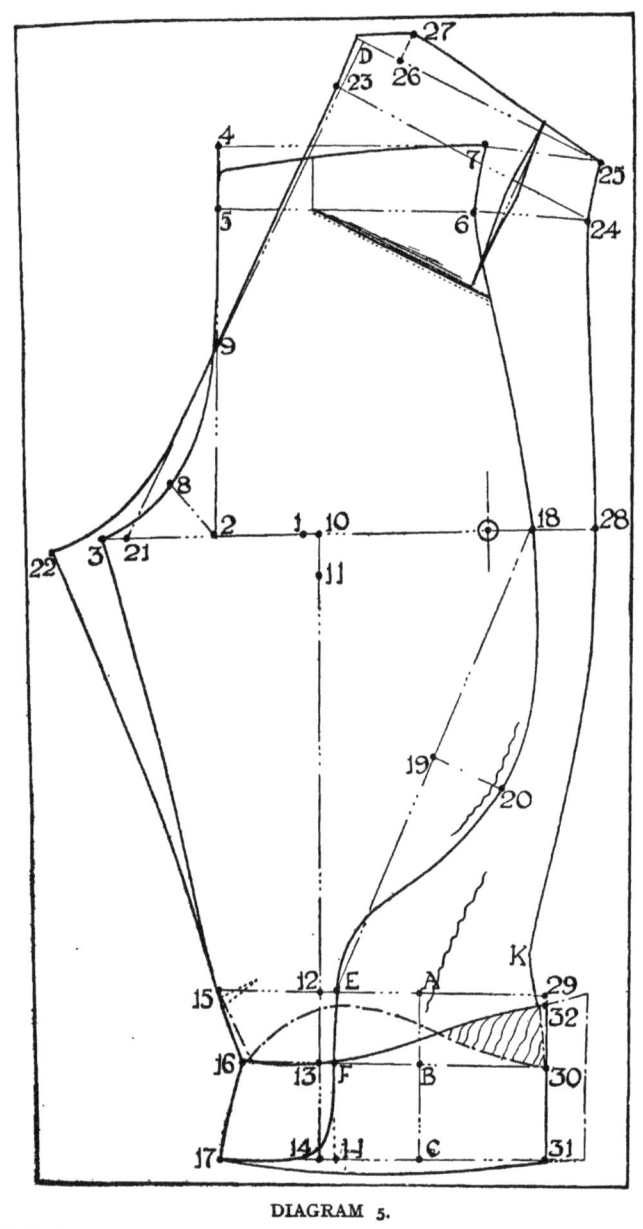

RIDING BREECHES

DIAGRAM 5.

RIDING BREECHES

24 from 23 = half waist plus 1½" (9½).
Spring out from 24 to 25.
D is located by squaring to 25 by the seat line.
26 from D = 2";
27 from 26 = 1¼";
Shape top as shown.
Take out a cut of ¼" in the waist;
Apply the knee width plus 1" (14½") from E to 15 and from 15 out to 29;
Apply the small width plus 1" (13") from F to 16 and from 16 to 30;
Apply the calf width plus 1" (13½") from H to 17 and from 17 to 31.
28 from 18 = 2½";
32 from 29 = ¾";
Shape to 13 and 16;
Measure from 18 round the curve of side seam to E;
Apply the amount registered plus ¾" from 28 to locate upper seam of cut at 30;
Curve upper half of cut as shown, taking 2" out above 13;
Hook the leg seam in at 16 (dot and dash lines), to make the length of the upper part of the seam agree with the lower half.
When shaping side-seam curve in at K to compare with the outline of topside above E.

Notes on the Draft

Provision for corpulency will only be affected at 5 and 4 as in trousers.
No provision for fulling at knee is made in this draft, and unless the fastening is arranged at the side of the leg, none is required.
The small knee cut below 15 in the topsides is only possible where strappings are to be worn.
Before joining the side-seams, the undersides must be shrunk to a nice hollow in the region of A (see wavy line).

TOP AND KNEE FINISHES. Diagram 6

THIS diagram has been devoted to illustrations of various top and knee finishes which are frequently asked for in Breeches Trades. With the diagrams and details given below the student should not experience any difficulty when it becomes necessary to infuse any of these style details into the full draft, already given in the last section.

Split Falls. Section A

This little sketch depicts the upper section of a pair of breeches finished with Split Falls. If referred to when the various parts have been cut out, it will help those unacquainted with the style in the checking up of the parts and show how they are assembled.
In the sketch the "fall" is shown detached from the buttons and laid over, exposing the inside finish.

Section B

This illustrates the preliminary trimming of the tops and the construction of the slit-bearer. The dash lines 1 and 2 represent the waist line.
The top of the "fall" runs ¼" above this line and extends 2¼" from 3 to 4.
The top side is slit down to a depth of 6" from 4 to 5 for the "fall."
Point 5 is situated 3¼" from the fly or front line.
The remaining section of the top-side is cut away ¼" above the waist line as from 6 to 7.
8 from 2 is 3" for the depth of the pocket.
9 from 8 = 6" for the pocket mouth.
The front bearer is shown by dot and dash lines extending from 6 out to 10.
10 from 1 = 1";
11 from 10 = 2¼";
Curve the bearer from 11 down to 5 as shown.

RIDING BREECHES

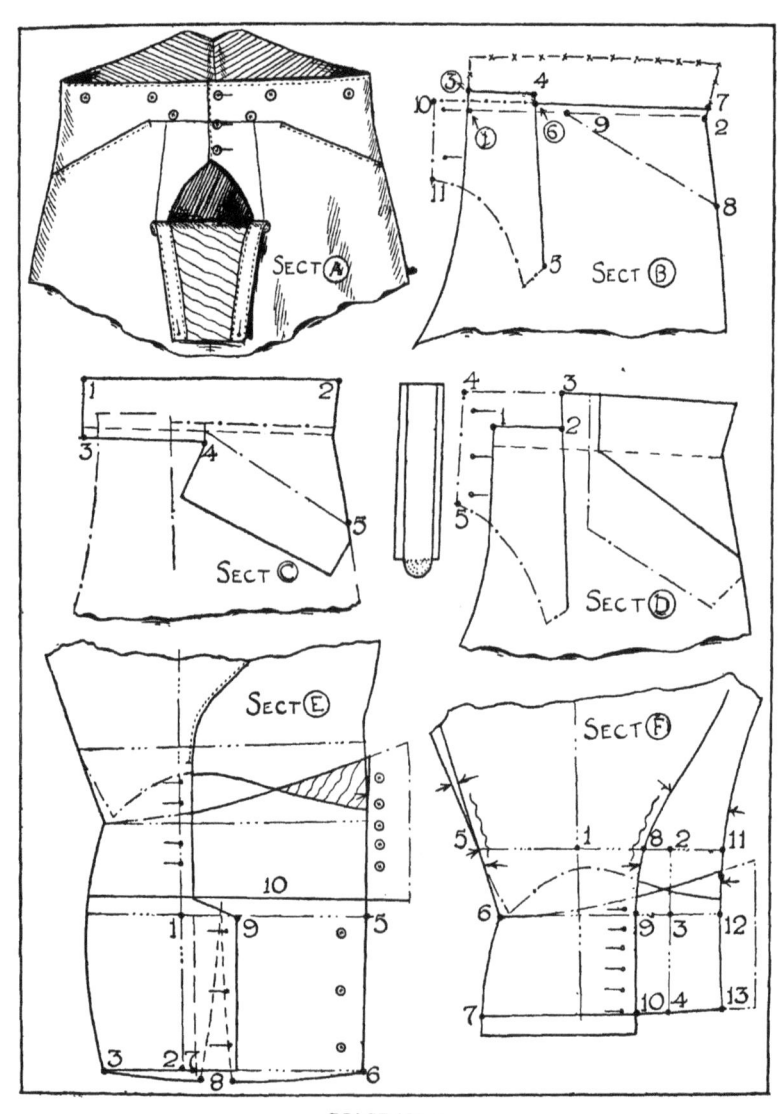

DIAGRAM 6.

RIDING BREECHES

Section C

This illustrates the cutting of the top and pocket bearer. Dot and dash lines show the outline of trimmed topside. This bearer, which is carried up to complete the height of the tops at 1 and 2, is extended ¼" beyond the front line.

A seam is allowed below the waist line from 3 to 4 and the pocket extension made below 4 and 5 as shown by solid line.

A welt cut to finish ¾" to 1" wide is constructed to be sewn down the side of the fall.

Section D

This depicts an alternative method of constructing Split Falls. Here the ordinary cross pocket is given, the facing and bearer being cut in accordance with the details laid down in the trousers section.

The front part of the topside is trimmed so that the "fall" 1 to 2 lies ¼" above the waist line.

The bearer is then cut to come right to the top as shown by dot and dash lines at 3, 4, and 5.

Continuations. Section E

This forms an extension of the breeches down below the calf, to a distance which is generally arranged to accord with the wishes of the customer.

The upper section at knee, small and calf is constructed as described in the full draft given previously.

2 from 1 is the extra length.

3 from 2 = ¼ the bottom measure.

Note.—The length of the continuation must be taken into account when measuring.

6 is squared down from 5.

Apply the full bottom measure plus 1" from 7 to 3 and from 3 out towards 6. Any surplus is taken out in a dart as shown at 8 (dash lines).

In order to prevent pressure of the buttons on the shin bone, the topsides are carried over to the side as shown at 9.

The continuations may be left on with the upper part, or they may be cut away on line 10 and made up in linen.

Fastening at Side of Knee. Section F

This diagram shows the altered outline of the breeches when the fastening has been arranged at the side of the knee.

2 from 1 = ¼ knee width;

3 and 4 are squared down from 2;

5 from 2 = half knee;

6 from 3 = half small;

7 from 4 = half calf;

8, 9, and 10 are placed 2" out from the centre line at 1;

Apply knee measure plus 1" from 8 to 5 and from 5 to 11;

Apply small plus 1" from 9 to 6 and 6 to 12;

Apply calf plus 1" from 10 to 7 and 7 to 13.

The overlap for the cut is found as before. With the seam coming down the side of the leg, it is necessary to infuse a little fullness on either side of topside knee to provide for the kneebone. This is accomplished by extending the topside ¼" below 7 and 10, and the placing of balance marks 3" apart on the underside and 3½" on the topside as shown by arrows.

GENTLEMEN'S GARMENT CUTTING

By PERCIVAL THICKETT

(Author of "Defects and Remedies," "Body Coats," etc.)

VEST CUTTING

S.B. AND D.B. STYLES. BY A PROPORTIONATE SYSTEM.

Diagram 7

FEATURES.—*Single breasted. No collar. Medium points and opening.*

MEASURES.—*36" breast; 32" waist; 16½" waist length; 12" opening; 25½" full length.*

INSTRUCTIONS FOR DRAFTING

IN this draft all the points are found by taking fractional quantities of a scale, which is derived from the circumference of breast measure.

The scale in this instance is 18" and is found by taking one-third the breast measure and adding 6". This formula obtains in all sizes from 36 upwards; but below 36 half breast gives the scale—i.e.—36 B = 18 scale; 42 B = 20 scale; 32 B = 16 scale—and so on.

No special provision is made for irregular figures in the working of the system, all deviations being made from the standard outline when marking out on the material.

S.B. VEST. SECTION A

Square lines from 0.
1 from 0 = half scale (9");
2 from 0 = waist length (16½");
3 from 2 = 1"; join to 0;
4 from 3 = ½";
Curve centre seam from 0 to 5 and down through 4;
6 from 0 = one-sixth scale plus ¼";
7 from 6 = ¾";
Draw back neck to 0;
8 from 0 is one-fourth the distance 0 to 1 (2¼");
Square out;

9 from 8 = one-third scale plus 1¾" (7¾");
10 is located by squaring down from 9;
11 from 5 = one-fourth full breast size, plus 1" (10);
12 from 5 = half breast plus 1½";
13 from 11 = one-twelfth scale plus ½": square up;
14 from 13 = one-sixth scale (3): square up;
15 from 14 = half scale (9);
Join 15 to 9;
16 from 15 is ⅜" less than the back shoulder seam from 7 to 9.

VEST CUTTING

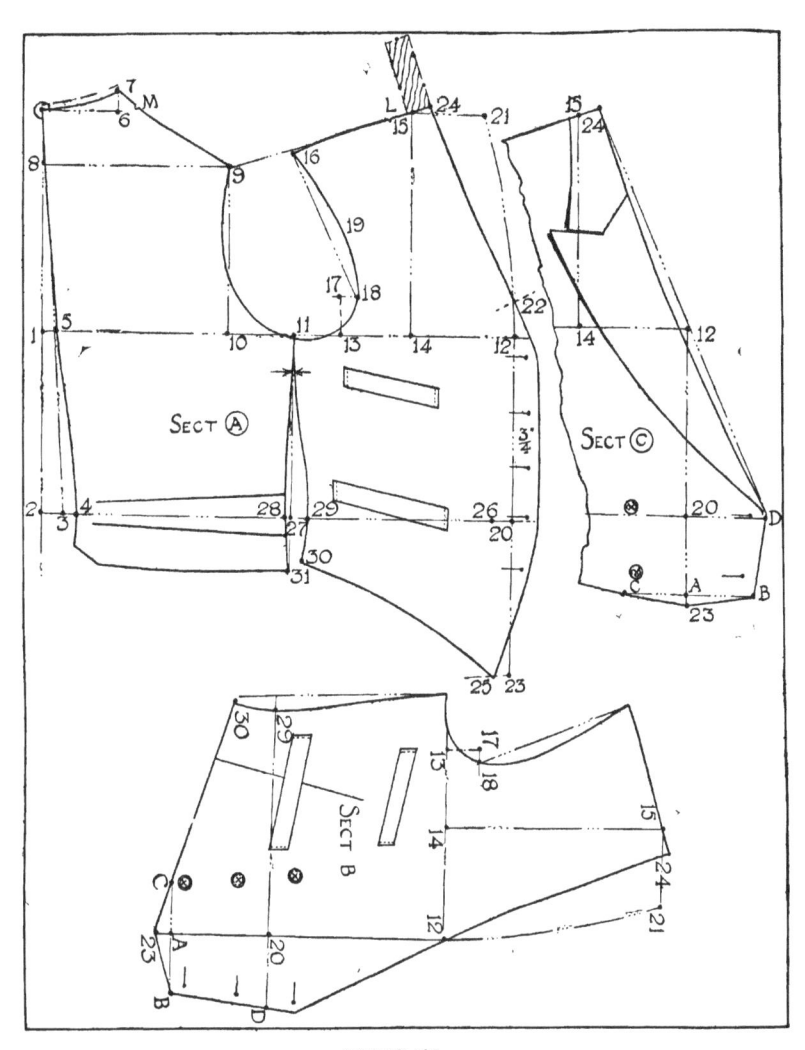

DIAGRAM 7

Drop ¼″ below the line;
17 from 13 = 1½″;
18 from 17 = ¾″: join to 16;
Shape scye hollowing ¼″ at 19, dropping ¼″ below breast line and hollowing ¼″ behind line from 10.

20 is found by squaring down from 12 in all instances where there is a difference of not less than 3″ between the breast and waist.
21 from 15 = one-sixth scale;
Curve line to 12;

VEST CUTTING

22 from 15 (by sweep) is the opening measure plus ¼" and less back neck 0 to 6;
23 from 15 (direct) = full length measure plus 1" and less the distance 0 to 6;
24 is a continuation of the shoulder and is ¾" out from 15;
25 is 1" from 23. This distance will vary to accord with the shape of the points desired.
Shape from point 24 through 22 and down to 25 extending ¾" beyond centre line for button stand.
26 from 4 = half waist plus 1¾";
27 is squared down from 11;
28 from 27 = ¼";
29 from 28 = the waist surplus shown at 26 to 20.
Shape side seams as shown, making 30, 2" to 2½" below the waist line and the back at 31, ½" lower.
The back neck piece, which is usually cut on the crease edge of the material, is sewn on at 24.
The exact run of this is shown by the shaded portion between dot and dash lines.
The lower pocket is 5" to 5½" in length, and its position 1" away from the side seam, 3½" from the bottom at the rear end and 5" at the front.
The top pockets are placed 5" above the lower ones and made 3½" to 4½" wide.

D.B. No-Collar Vest.
Section B

This diagram depicts the full length double-breasted shape with a no-collar finish.
The back section remains the same and the numbers, which correspond to those given in the previous draft, are found as described for that vest.
23 is the full length to measure.
A is ¼" up from 23;
Square out on either side;
B from A = 2¼": C from A is the same.
D from 20 = 3 to 3½";
Draw from B through D and curve bottom run through C;
The opening is continued from 24 through 12 (or opening point) until it cuts the line up from D;
The lapel section in front of line 12-23 may be cut off and sewn on separately.
The distance between the line of buttons and the centre line is made ¾" less than the overlap given beyond 20 and A.

D.B. Collar Vest.
Section C

This diagram displays the new shape of the D.B. variety with a short and straight bottom run.
23 is 3¼" from 20;
A is ¾" above 23;
B from A = 2¼": C from A is the same;
D from 20 = 3¾";
Join D to 24 and hollow slightly as shown.
The collar, which is made up separately and sewn on, is shaped with a bold curve.
The position of the step should be located slightly lower than the midway point between the neck 15 and the breast line 14.
To give a better effect and to facilitate the making up, the upper section can be cut separately and joined on, thus forming a natural "break seam" similar to a coat.

Notes on the Draft

The indifferent manner in which vests are often put together is chiefly the cause of the badly wrinkled shoulders of which customers so frequently complain.
Balance marks should therefore be placed at the shoulders L and M, and also in the side seams, for the guidance of the work-hand.
When chalking round the back on the Italian, a small turning-up allowance should be left at back neck, as outlined by dot and dash lines.
When sewing the back centre seam, the stitching should come ¼" inside the pattern line. Facings are frequently left on down the opening edge (12 to 24), when cutting from the cloth. When this is done, the work-hand must be instructed to turn the edge so that the thread marks lie ¼" inside and not on the line of edge, as is so frequently done.

VEST CUTTING

DRESS VEST BY DIRECT MEASURES. Diagram 8

FEATURES :—*Single-breasted. Roll collar. Semi-vee opening. Three buttons.*

MEASURES :—36" breast ; 32" waist ; 9" scye depth ; 16½" waist length ; 12¾" front shoulder ; 17¾" over shoulder ; full length and opening to style.

NOTE.—The front shoulder has been made ¼" and the across chest ½" less than the measures taken over the lounge jacket.

INSTRUCTIONS FOR DRAFTING

IN this draft the application of the short direct measures is shown. The great virtue of this system lies in the complete manner in which it provides for irregular figures direct on the draft, without the use of judgment.

The construction of the draft for dress vests is practically the same as for the ordinary no-collar type, the only variation being at the front.

There are many varieties of front finish, but the selection given here has been confined to the more standard shapes.

The working scale 18 is found as explained in the previous draft.

ROLL COLLAR VEST. SECTION A
Square lines from 0.
1 from 0 = scye depth 9" ;
2 from 0 = waist length 16½";
3 from 2 = 1" : join to 0 ;
4 from 3 = ½" ;
Shape back seam from A ;
5 from 1 = one-third the over-shoulder measure plus ¾" ;
Square out ;
6 from 5 = one-third scale plus 1¼" (7¾") ;
7 from 0 = one-sixth scale plus ¼" (3¼") ;
8 from 7 = ¾" ;
Shape to 0 and join to 6.
9 is squared down from 6 ;
10 from A = one-fourth breast plus 1" ;
11 from A = half breast plus 1½" ;
12 from 11 = across chest measure 7½" ;
13 from 12 = one-sixth scale ;
Square up ;
Deduct the width of back neck 0 to 7 from the front shoulder measure and sweep the remainder from 12 through line 13 as shown by 14.
Deduct ¼" from the over-shoulder measure and apply the remainder from A to B (centre of shoulder) and from 12 to 15 by a sweep.
15 from 14 = 8 to 6 less ⅜" ;
16 from 12 = 1½" ;
17 from 16 = ¾" ;
Join to 15 ;
Shape the armhole hollowing ¼" at 18 ; dropping ¼" below 10 and up ¼" behind line 9 to 6 ;
19 is squared down from 11 for all sizes where the waist is 3" or more less than the breast.
20 from 19 is the length desired, in this instance 5¼".
21 from 20 = 1" ;
Add ¾" beyond centre line 19 for button stand and fix the opening 1½" to 2" up from the waist at 22.
C is ¾" out from 14 ;
Connect to 22 and hollow the neck 1" ;

23

VEST CUTTING

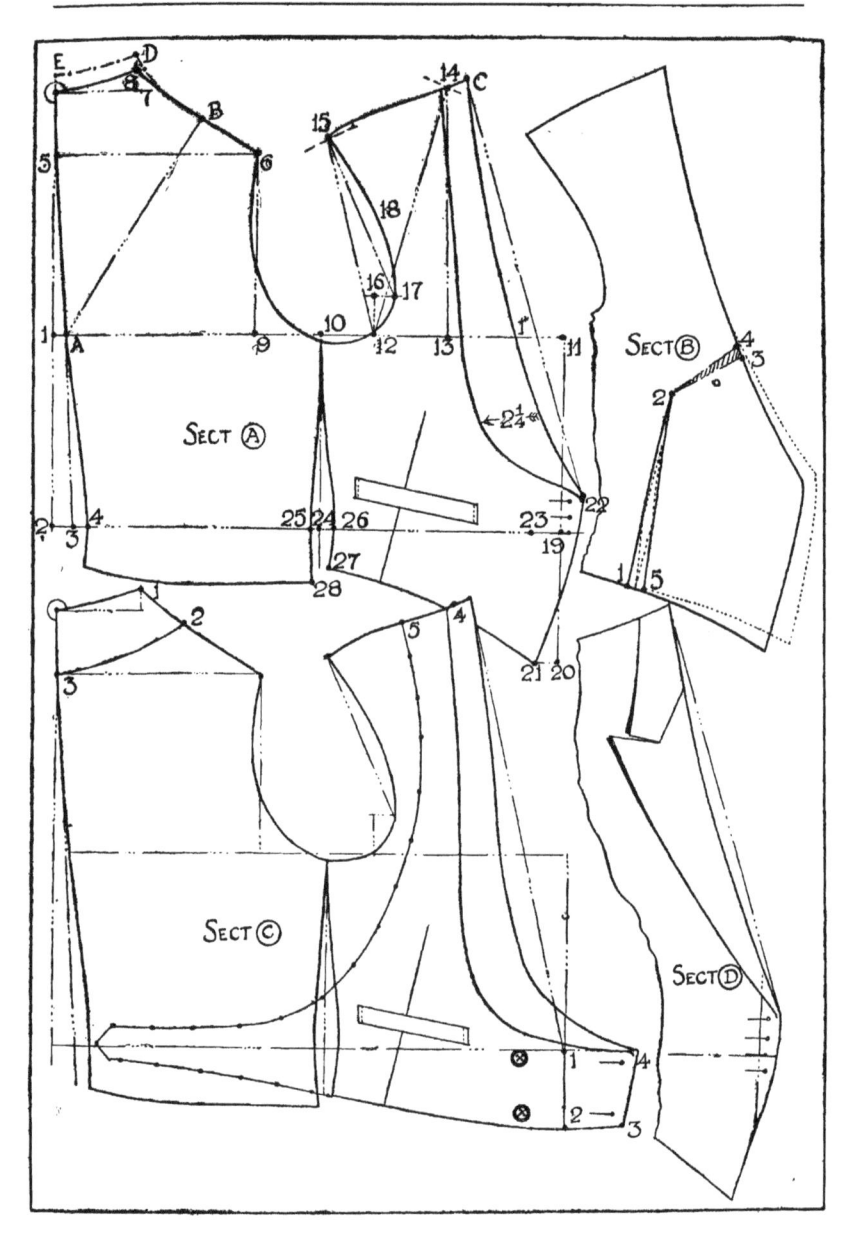

DIAGRAM 8.

VEST CUTTING

23 from 4 = half waist plus 1½";
24 is squared down from 10;
25 is ¼" from 24;
26 from 25 = the waist surplus shown from 23 to 19.
27 from 26 = 1½";
28 is ¼" lower than 27;
Shape side seam as shown giving a little spring at the bottom.

MANIPULATION OF THE FRONT.
SECTION B

The manipulation of the pattern shown in this diagram has the twofold effect of giving an elegant-shaped waist for normal figures and providing a close sit at the opening. Both these features are essential to a good-fitting vest.
Cut the pattern upon the dart line from 1 to 2 as shown.
Pleat the front over ¼" to ½" at 3 and 4 and the forepart will swing forward as shown by dotted line. The dart is also opened from 1 to 5.
Shape the waist dart, filling in to a point midway between 1 and 5.
When chalking out on the cloth follow the dotted line at the front.

D.B. BACKLESS VEST. SECTION C

For this modern type of finish the draft is produced in ordinary manner as described above.
The back part is cut away to a narrow neck band as outlined by dotted lines at 1, 2, and 3.
The front shoulder is then shortened to meet the alteration in the back, 4 to 5 being the same distance as 2 to 3.
From 5 curve down the shoulder, well clear of the scye front, and on to the side waist. Here the forepart is extended to form an adjusting strap at back waist.
The front shown is the very popular D.B. buttoning two with a straight bottom run.
2 from 1 = 3";
3 from 2 = 2¾";
4 from 1 = 3½";
Join front to the neck and hollow 1" as shown.

VEE-SHAPED POINTED LAPEL.
SECTION D

This is another popular front finish with the opening carried straight to the first buttonhole. The collar shown is the ordinary pointed step.

NOTES ON THE DRAFT

In order to dispense with the carrying of the collar round to the back neck, the lining of the back can be extended right through to the top. The alteration necessary for this is shown by dot and dash lines at E and D, these two points being located ⅝" above o and 8.
From D run gradually out into the shoulder seam as shown.
Provision for increased waist size will be shown in a later draft.

PLATE III

HAWKES & CO., LTD., SAVILE ROW, LONDON, W.1. CUTTING HALL.

GENTLEMEN'S GARMENT CUTTING

By PERCIVAL THICKETT

(*Author of "Defects and Remedies," "Body Coats," etc.*)

COAT CUTTING

S.B. LOUNGE. BY A PROPORTIONATE SYSTEM. Diagram 9

FEATURES :—*Single-breasted ; step collar ; button three ; seam back ; moderately high and shaped waist.*

MEASURES :—*36" breast ; 32" waist ; 38" seat ; 7" back width ; 16½" waist length ; 29" full length. Scale 18".*

INSTRUCTIONS FOR DRAFTING

THE formula for finding the scale (18") is the same as explained for the vest. The draft can be worked out direct on the cloth by first of all constructing the back section, then cutting it out and laying it in a convenient position.

The back has a seam (¼") allowed down the centre, so where an inlay is allowed, special instructions should be given to the work-hand to sew a quarter-inch inside the chalk line.

The shape of the front in this draft is not standard and can be varied to button two or only one by lowering the crease line of the lapel.

The breast cut at 32 is optional, but should be included when a close-fitting waist is desired. This particular dart should be sewn in the chalk lines ; that at 31, ¼" inside the line.

SECTION A

Square lines from o.
1 from o = half scale (9") ;
2 from o = waist length, 16¼", less the amount the waist is required above the natural.
3 from 2 = 1 to 2 plus 1½" ;
4 from o = full length ;
5 from 2 = ¾" : join to o ;
6 from 5 = ¾" ;
Curve gradually into o 5 line ;

7 from 4 = 1¼" ;
8 from o = one-fourth the distance o to 1 ; square out ;
9 from 8 = 2¾" in sizes 36 and above ; Below 36 breast 9 is made one-fourth scale plus ¼" from o ;
10 from the inside line at 9 = back width plus ½" for two seams.
11 and 12 are located by squaring from 10 by 9 ;
13 from 12 = ½" ;

COAT CUTTING

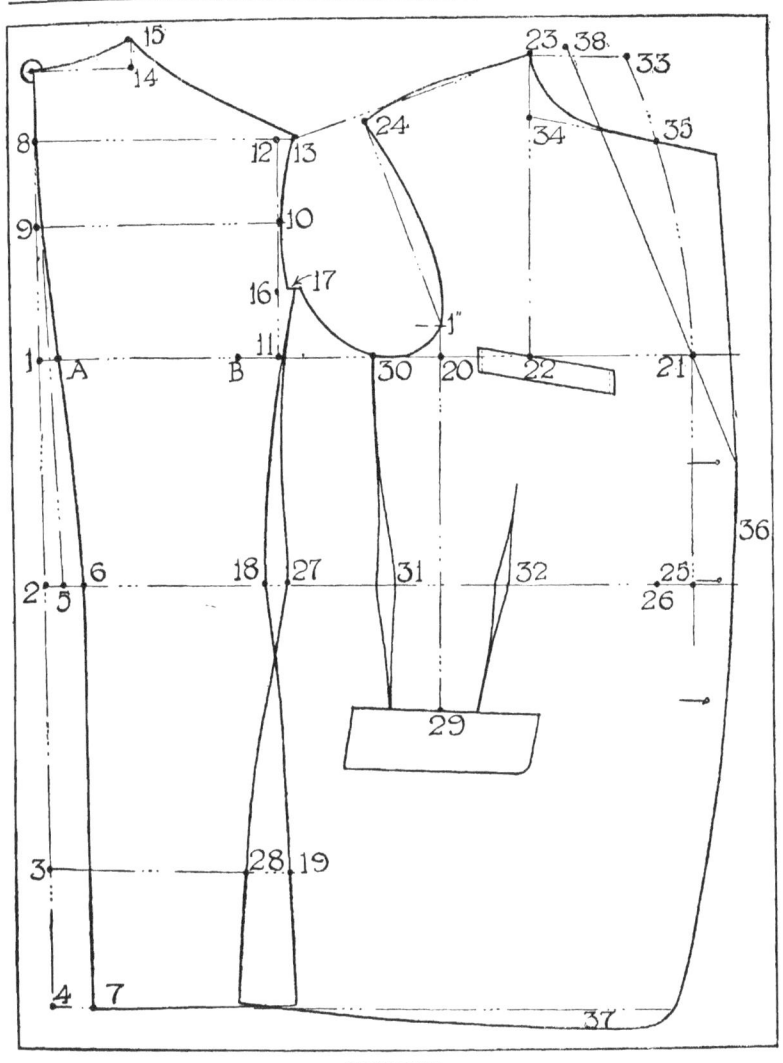

DIAGRAM 9.

This amount can be varied if a wider or narrower shoulder is desired.
14 from 0 = one-sixth scale plus ¼″ (3¼″);
15 from 14 = ¾″;
Join to 0 for back neck.

16 from 11 = 2″;
17 from 16 = ¼″;
Mark a ¼″ each way for seams from this point and shape back scye.
18 from 6 = 1″ less than back width (6″);

T. I—4

COAT CUTTING

19 from 3 = 2 to 18 plus $\frac{1}{4}''$;
Shape the side seam from 17 through 18 and down through 19, curving slightly below 18.
B from A = one-third half breast (6");
20 from B = $\frac{1}{4}$ half breast plus 2" (6$\frac{1}{2}$);
21 from A = half breast plus 2$\frac{1}{2}''$;
22 from 20 = one-sixth scale;
Square up.
23 from 22 = half scale plus $\frac{1}{4}''$;
Join 23 to 13;
24 from 23 = 13 to 15 less $\frac{1}{4}''$;
Drop $\frac{1}{4}''$ below line;
Mark up 1" from 20 and join to 24;
Shape shoulder, giving a slight curve, and the scye, hollowing $\frac{1}{2}''$ below 24;
25 is found by squaring down from 21 for sizes where the waist is not less than 3" smaller than the breast.
26 from 6 = half the waist measure plus 2$\frac{1}{2}''$;
27 from 18 = half the waist surplus shown between points 25 and 26;
28 from 19 = the difference between the half breast and half seat measures plus $\frac{1}{2}''$ (1$\frac{1}{2}$);
Curve forepart side seam through 27 and 28, giving a slight round over the hip.
29 is the centre of pocket and is located by squaring down 11" to 12" from 20.
Make the width of pocket 6$\frac{1}{4}''$;
30 from 20 = 2$\frac{1}{4}''$;
Shape the underarm dart to rear end of pocket, suppressing the waist at 31 one-half the waist surplus shown from 25 to 26.
The breast dart runs at a forward incline from the front end of the pocket and for proportionate figures should not be suppressed more than $\frac{1}{4}''$ at 32.
33 from 23 = one-sixth scale;
Curve down to 21;
34 from 23 = 2";
35 from 33 = one-sixth scale;
Join to 34.
Shape the neck, hollowing to within 1" of 34.
Add 1$\frac{1}{2}''$ beyond the centre line at 36 and extend the bottom of forepart $\frac{3}{4}''$ below bottom construction line at 37;
38 for crease line is 1" out from 23;
Draw the crease line to the front edge as shown.

NOTES ON THE DRAFT

In trades that cater for manual workers it may be found advisable to advance point 20 at the front of scye and the neck line at 22 to accommodate the muscular shoulder development in such figures.

For an easier fitting waist section the front dart will be left out and only a proportion of the waist surplus (26 to 25) will be taken out at the underarm dart and side seam.

Point 24 will vary in its position slightly to accord with the amount of wadding introduced and the degree of manipulation that the shoulder will be subject to.

The line 34 to 35 has only to be considered from a point of view of style and can be varied.

COAT CUTTING

D.B. REEFER. BY DIRECT MEASURES. Diagram 10

FEATURES :—*Double-breasted fronts, buttoning two and showing three ; moderately high and close-fitting waist ; jetted hip pockets ; welted outside breast pocket.*
MEASURES :—36" *breast ;* 32" *waist ;* 38" *seat ;* 9" *scye depth ;* 16½" *waist length ;* 28¾" *full length ;* 13" *front shoulder ;* 17¾" *over-shoulder ;* 8" *across chest ;* 7" *across back. Scale* 18".

INSTRUCTIONS FOR DRAFTING

THE application of the direct measures to the ordinary S.B. Lounge will be identical with the procedure explained in this draft. The neck has been lowered to suit the particular style of step and the increased length of lapel. The overlap for the buttons is a variable feature and should be arranged in accordance with the build of the man.

BODY PART. SECTION A
Square lines from o.
1 from o = scye depth (9") ;
2 from o = waist length less, say, ¼" for the fashionable line.
3 from 2 = 1 to 2 plus 1½" ;
4 from o = full length plus making-up allowance.
5 from 2 = ¾" : join to o.
6 from 5 = ¾" ;
Curve gradually into the above line, above the breast line.
7 from 4 = 1¼" : complete back seam.
8 from 1 = one-third over-shoulder measure plus ¾" : square out ;
9 from 8 = 2¼" : square out ;
10 from inside line at 9 = back width plus ¼" ;
Points 11 and 12 are located by squaring by line 9 to 10 ;
13 from 12 = ¼" or more if a wider shoulder is desired.
14 from o = one-sixth scale plus ¼" ; square up ;
15 from 14 = ¾" ;
Shape to o and to 13 ;
16 is 2" above 11 ;
17 is ¼" out from 16 for side seam ;
Mark ¼" each way for seam.
18 from 6 = back width less 1" (6") ;

19 from 3 = 2 to 18 plus ½" ;
Shape side seam of back as shown through 18 and 19 ;
20 from A = half breast plus 2½" ;
21 from 20 = across chest 8" ;
22 from 21 = one-sixth scale (3") ; square up.
23 by sweep from 21 = front shoulder measure less back neck o to 14 ;
Apply the over-shoulder measure less ¼" from A to 24 and then from 21 to 25 by sweeping.
25 is definitely located by applying the width of back shoulder seam (15 to 13) less ¼" from 23.
Join 25 to 1" up from 21 ;
Hollow scye ½" ;
26 is squared down from 20 ;
27 from 6 = half waist plus 2½" ;
28 from 18 = half the waist surplus shown from 26 to 27.
29 from 19 = half the difference between the breast and seat measures plus ½".
30 is 2" from 21 for underarm seam ;
Square down to B from 21 for centre of pocket.
Shape underarm dart to rear of pocket, taking out half the waist surplus (26 to 27) at 31 ;
32 is the breast dart : take out ¼" ;

COAT CUTTING

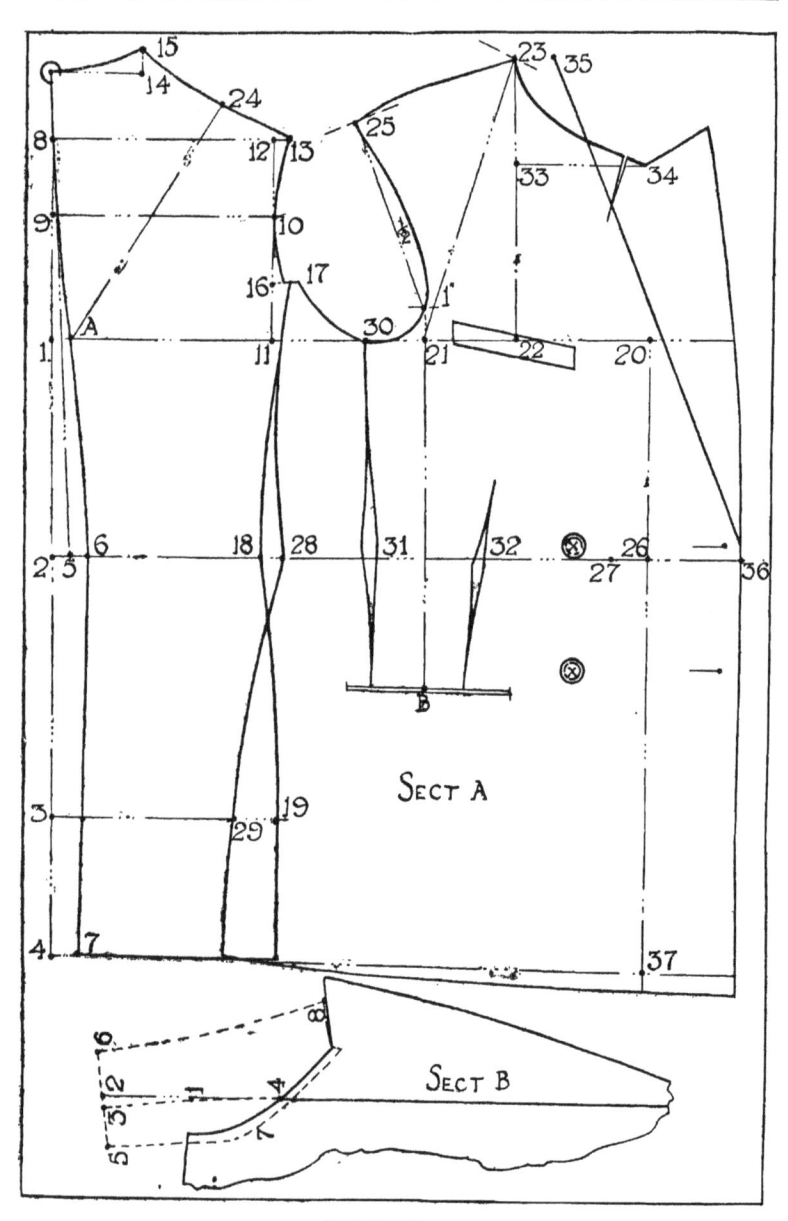

DIAGRAM 10.

COAT CUTTING

33 from 23 = one-sixth scale plus ½" (3½");

Square out for end of lapel step at 34.

35 for crease row is 1" out from 23;

Allow 3" to 4" from 26 to 36 for the overlap, and shape front as shown.

Extend the bottom of forepart ¾" below bottom construction line at 37, and keep a straight run for a distance equal to twice the frontage given (26 to 36).

The vertical spacing of the buttons is arranged so that the lower set comes in line with the pocket. The distance back from the centre line is ¾" less than the amount of overlap on the front.

COLLAR CUTTING. SECTION B

The solid line shows the outline of the neck.

Point 35 in the big draft is represented here by point 1.

2 from 1 = 0 to 14 of neck.

3 from 2 = ¼" for spring;

Curve to 4.

Using line 3 to 4 as guide, square back of collar 5 and 6.

5 from 3 = 1¼", the "stand";

6 from 3 = 2", the "fall";

Curve the stand to follow the outline of the neck, allowing ¼" as shown at 7.

8 is arranged to agree with the style of step desired.

Where the collar is to be turned in previous to being felled, or where it is sewn on by machine, add ¼" round the stand: curve 5 to 7.

NOTES ON THE DRAFT

The instructions for giving ease to the scye laid down in the last draft can very well be ignored here, as the across chest should automatically regulate the position of the scye to accord with the build of the figure.

When the measures have been carefully taken, no further adjustment should be required for short or long-necked figures, sloping or square shoulders, or erectness of carriage.

COAT CUTTING

THE SLEEVE DRAFT. Diagram 11

THE sleeve system demonstrated here is based on measurements taken from the scye. Therefore, if there is any variation from the normal shape produced in the drafting of the body part, these changes are automatically transferred to the sleeve draft.

The marking of both the pitches before the garment is sent out to the work-hand and checking up when it is returned is most strongly advised. Indifferent pitching of the sleeves in the workshop is largely responsible for the unsightly fullness at the hindarm of which customers so frequently complain.

Position of the Pitches
Section A

Point 1 in this section depicts the portion of the back pitch. In all sizes 36 breast and above this is located by squaring from point 2, which is $2\frac{3}{4}''$ from 3.

Below 36 breast point 2 should be situated half A B plus $\frac{1}{4}''$ from A.

The front pitch at 4 is located $\frac{3}{4}''$ above the breast line 5;

7 from 6 on the back line is the same distance as 5 to 4.

The Sleeve. Section B

Square lines from 0.

1 from 0 = 1 to 7 of scye plus $\frac{3}{4}''$;
2 direct from 1 = the upper half of the scye as shown by wavy line from 1 to 8 and 9 to 4.
3 is midway between 0 and 2;
4 from 3 = 1 to 8 less $1\frac{1}{4}''$.
5 is midway between 3 and 0.
Shape the crown of the sleeve from 1 through 5 and 4 and on to 2.
6 is the sleeve length and is found by applying the length measured less the netback width from 2 (31'' minus 7'').
7 from 6 = $1\frac{1}{2}''$; square out;
8 from 7 direct = one-third scale (as for coat) plus $\frac{1}{4}''$;
9 from 1 = half 1 to 6 less $\frac{1}{2}''$;
Square out for elbow line.
10 from 9 = 1'';
Connect to 6 and 1;
11 from 10 = one-third scale plus 2''.
This completes the top side.

For Underside 12 from 1 direct = the lower half of the scye (round the curve) from 1 to 4.

13 from 1 = half 5 to 6, the scye width.

Allow $\frac{1}{4}''$ at 1 and 12 for seams and curve through 13, sinking $\frac{1}{4}''$ below the line from 1.

The sleeve drafted in this fashion will allow a reasonable amount of fullness over the crown.

The underpart should be well eased in the region of the wavy line when putting the sleeve into the scye.

Three-quarter Sleeve
Section C

This is popularly known as the "false forearm" finish and is introduced to bring the forearm seam well under the arm and out of sight.

Points 1, 5, and 8 would be the track of the seam as shown in the preceding draft.

The underside is curtailed 1'' as shown at 2, 6, and 9, $\frac{1}{4}''$ being allowed from 2 to 3 for the seam.

4 is opposite point 3 and is 1'' from 1.

7 from 5 and 10 from 8 are also 1''.

Point 10 is slightly higher than 9; this allows for the stretching which is necessary in the region of 7 to get the sleeve to lie over nicely.

Split Pivot Sleeve. Section D

This is a novel but very useful arrangement which provides a superabundance of ease when the arms are in

COAT CUTTING

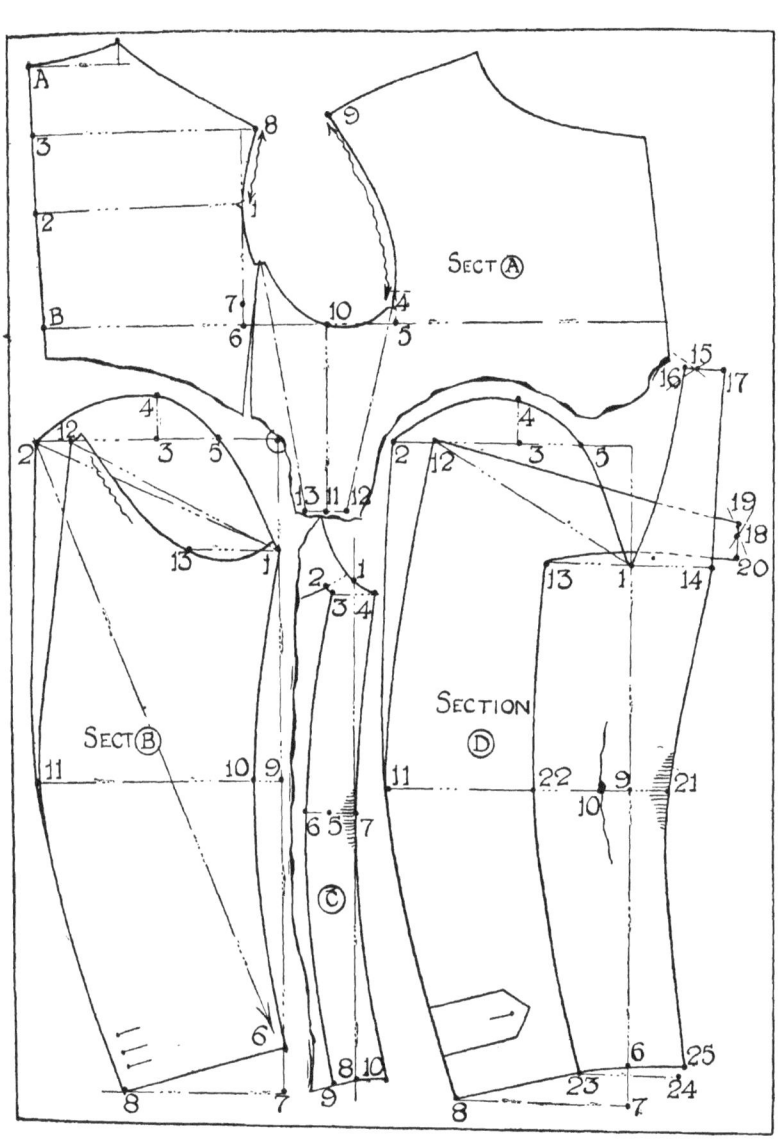

DIAGRAM 11.

action, and is chiefly confined to sporting coats, such as are used for shooting and golfing.

Instead of the ordinary shaped underside, a wedge-shaped piece is introduced, to be sewn under the arms and down the side of the coat. The finished appearance is very much like the ordinary sleeve, excepting that a deep pleat is formed in the underside at back scye.

The outline of the wedge-shaped piece is shown on Section A by dot and dash lines.

This is marked for the guidance of the work-hands, but must not be cut away.

10 from 5 = half 5 to 6 less $\frac{1}{2}''$;
11 from 10 can be arranged to taste.
12 and 13 are each $\frac{1}{2}''$ from 11;
Shape as shown.

Sleeve Draft

Points 1 to 11 are located as described in Section B for the ordinary sleeve.

12 from 1 = the lower scye quantity 4, 10 to 1;
13 from 1 = 5 to 10 plus $\frac{1}{2}''$;
14 from 1 is the same.

To locate point 15 take the distance 4 to 12 and sweep from 1; also the distance from 10 to 11 plus $\frac{1}{2}''$ and sweep from 14.

16 from 15 = $\frac{1}{4}''$;
17 from 15 = 11 to 12 plus $\frac{1}{4}''$;
Join 16 to 1 and 17 to 14.

To locate 18 take the distance 1 to 13 (direct) and sweep from 12; also the distance 10 to 11 plus $\frac{1}{2}''$, and sweep from 13.

19 from 18 = $\frac{1}{4}''$;
20 from 18 = 11 to 13 plus $\frac{1}{4}''$.
21 and 22 are each $2\frac{1}{2}''$ from 10.
23 and 24 are each $2''$ from 6.
25 from 24 = $\frac{1}{2}''$ to allow for stretching necessary in the region of 21.

When making, 17, 14, 21, and 25 are sewn to 20, 13, 22, and 23.

12 to 19 is turned in and stitched down on 1 to 13 of body part; in a like manner 1 to 16 goes to 4 and 12, on forepart.

DRESS LOUNGE. (SEMI-CORPULENT FIGURE.) Diagram 12

FEATURES :—*Single-breasted ; link front ; silk-faced lapels ; jetted hip and welted outside breast pockets ; close hips and shapely waist.*

MEASURES :—40″ *breast ;* 40″ *waist ;* 42″ *seat ;* 9¾″ *scye depth ;* 17¼″ *waist length ;* 29½″ *full length ;* 13⅞″ *front shoulder ;* 18¾″ *over shoulder ;* 8¾″ *across chest ;* 8″ *across back. Scale* 19½″.

INSTRUCTIONS FOR DRAFTING

THIS draft illustrates how the waist is adjusted for figures slightly above normal. It is essential to have the amount of disproportion in order to regulate the distribution of the excess waist size. This is found by deducting 4″ from the breast measure and comparing the result with the actual waist size, viz. 40 B − 4 = 36″ : 36 from 40 W = 4″ disproportion.

The change from the ordinary to the dress lounge is very little and consists of reduction at the front overlap.

DRAFT

Square lines from o.
1 from o = scye depth 9¾″ ;
2 from o = waist length 17¼″ less ½″ for the fashion line.
3 from 2 = 2 to 1 plus 1½″ ;
4 from o = full length.
5 from 2 = ¾″ ; join to o.
6 from 5 = ¾″ : curve into line 5.
7 from 4 = 1¼″ ;
8 from o = one-sixth scale plus ¼″ ;
9 from 8 = ¾″ : shape to o.
10 from 1 = one-third over shoulder plus ¾″ :
11 from 10 = 2¾″ : square out from 10 and 11.
12 from 11 = back width plus ½″ ;
13 and 14 are located by squaring from 12.
15 from 14 = ½″ : join to 9.
16 from 13 = 2″ ;
17 from 16 = ½″ : mark ¼″ each side for seams.
18 from A = half breast plus 2½″ ;
19 from 18 = across chest 8¾″ ;
B from 18 = ⅛ disproportion less ¼″ ;
Join to 19.
20 from 19 on line to B = one-sixth scale : square up.
21 from 19 = front shoulder measure less back neck o to 8.
Apply the over-shoulder measure less ½″ from A to C and then from 19 to 22 by a sweep.
22 is definitely located by applying the back shoulder width 9 to 15 less ¼″ from 21.
Mark up 1″ from 19 and join to 22 ;
Hollow scye ½″ at 23.
24 from 6 = back width less 1″ (7″) ;
25 from 3 = 2 to 24 plus ½″ ;
26 is squared down from 18.
27 from 26 = one-fourth disproportion less ¼″ : join to 18.
28 from 6 = half the waist plus 2″
29 from 24 = half 28 to 27 ;
30 from 25 = half the difference between the breast and hip plus ½″ (1½″).
31 from 19 = 2½″ ;
C is squared down from 19 and is 11″ down.
Shape the underarm dart from 31 to rear of pocket, taking out half the waist surplus (28 to 27) at 32.
33 from 21 = one-sixth scale ;
34 from 21 = one-sixth scale ;
Curve to B.
Shape the lapel as shown from 21 on to line 23.
Add ¾″ beyond the centre line at 27 for the front edge and shape as shown to the bottom. Give ¾″

COAT CUTTING

below the bottom construction line at 35 and complete.

NOTES ON THE DRAFT

There are some figures which are very flat in the back waist and seat region. This will necessitate a slight adjustment in the distribution of the waist increment, a little more being placed at the front waist 27 and less at the side.

For the popular barrel effect the pattern can be pleated over at M (dot and dash lines) before being placed on the material. This will have the effect of opening the dart at 31. The space exposed will then be cut away in the material.

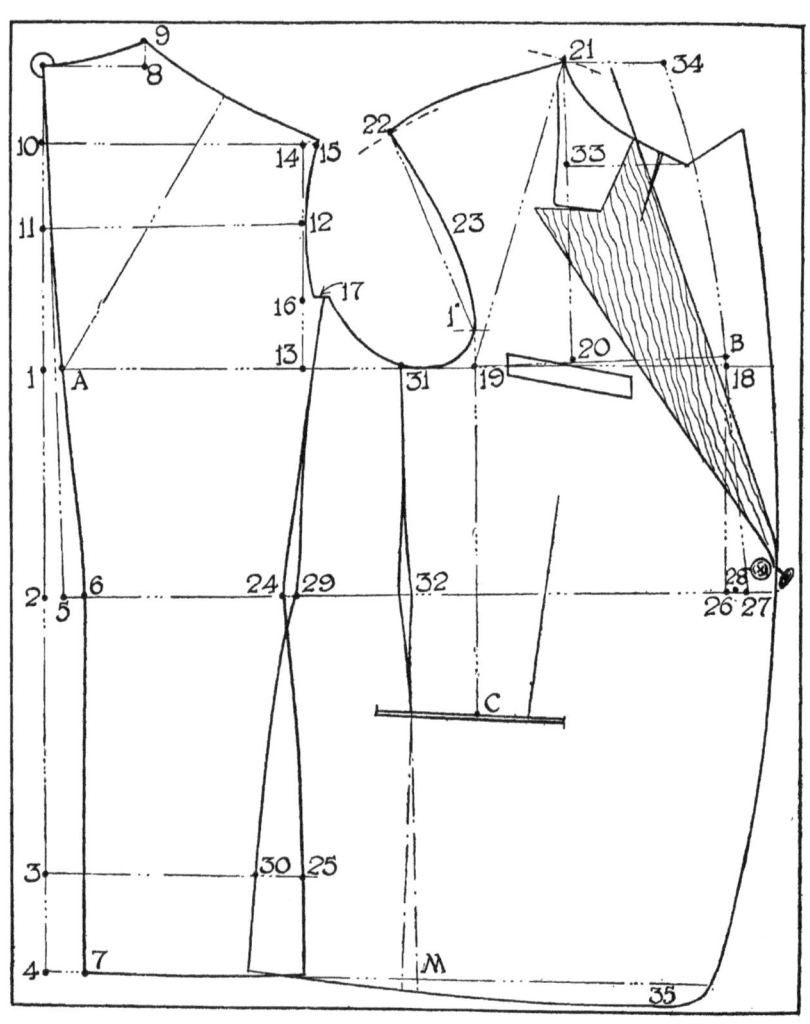

DIAGRAM 12.

COAT CUTTING

MORNING COAT. Diagram 13

FEATURES :—*Button one ; pointed lapel ; close waist ; high and straight waist seam. Cut-away skirt.*
MEASURES.—*36" breast ; 32" waist ; 38" seat ; 9" scye depth ; 16½" waist length ; 38½" full length ; 13" front shoulder ; 17¾" over shoulder ; 7" across back ; 8" across chest. Scale 18".*

INSTRUCTIONS FOR DRAFTING

THE scale for body-coats is found in the same way as for lounges.

The system shown for the construction of the draft is the Direct Measure one, but where the additional measures are not available, the proportionate arrangement, given previously, can be used.

The length of the waist between points 2 and 3 can be varied in accordance with the prevailing fashion.

The ordinary S.B. step collar can be used in place of the pointed one shown ; also the fronts may carry two or three buttons.

DRAFT

Square lines from o.
1 from o = scye depth 9" ;
2 from o = waist length 16½" ;
3 from 2 = 1" or to taste ;
4 from o = full length 38½" ;
5 from 2 = 1¼" : connect to o.
6 is squared down from 5.
7 from o = one-sixth scale plus ¼" ;
8 from 7 = ¾" : shape to o.
Mark out ¼" at 3 and square down for vent.
9 from 1 = one-third over shoulder plus ¾" : square out.
10 from 9 = 2¾" : square out.
11 from the inside line at 10 = back width plus ¼" ;
12 and 13 are squared from 11 ;
14 from 13 = ½" ;
Connect to 8 for shoulder seam.
15 from 5 = one-ninth scale (2"), but this can be made slightly larger where heavy tweeds are used.
Join 11 to 2 and shape the blade seam, giving 1" of round at 16.
Square down from 15 to B.
17 from A = half breast plus 2½"
18 from 17 = across chest 8";

19 from 18 = one-sixth scale (3") square up.
Sweep the front shoulder measure less back neck (0 to 7) from 18 to 20 ;
Deduct ¼" from the over-shoulder measure and apply from A to 21, then from 18 to 22, by a sweep.
22 is definitely located by applying the width of back shoulder 8 to 14, less ¼" from 20 to 22.
Mark up 1" from 18 and join to 22.
Hollow the scye ¼" in front of the construction line.
23 is squared down from 17 ;
24 from 5 = half waist plus 2" ;
25 from 15 = two-thirds the waist surplus shown from 24 to 23.
26 is 1½" from 12 : go up 1¼" for summit of underarm seam and mark a seam's width on either side.
27 from 25 = 16 to 26 less ¾" ;
28 from 27 = one-third the waist surplus (24 to 23).
When shaping the underarm seam give a little spring.
Using 11 as a pivot, sweep from B to C ;
From C square out the lower waist line to 29 (parallel with line 5 to 23).

COAT CUTTING

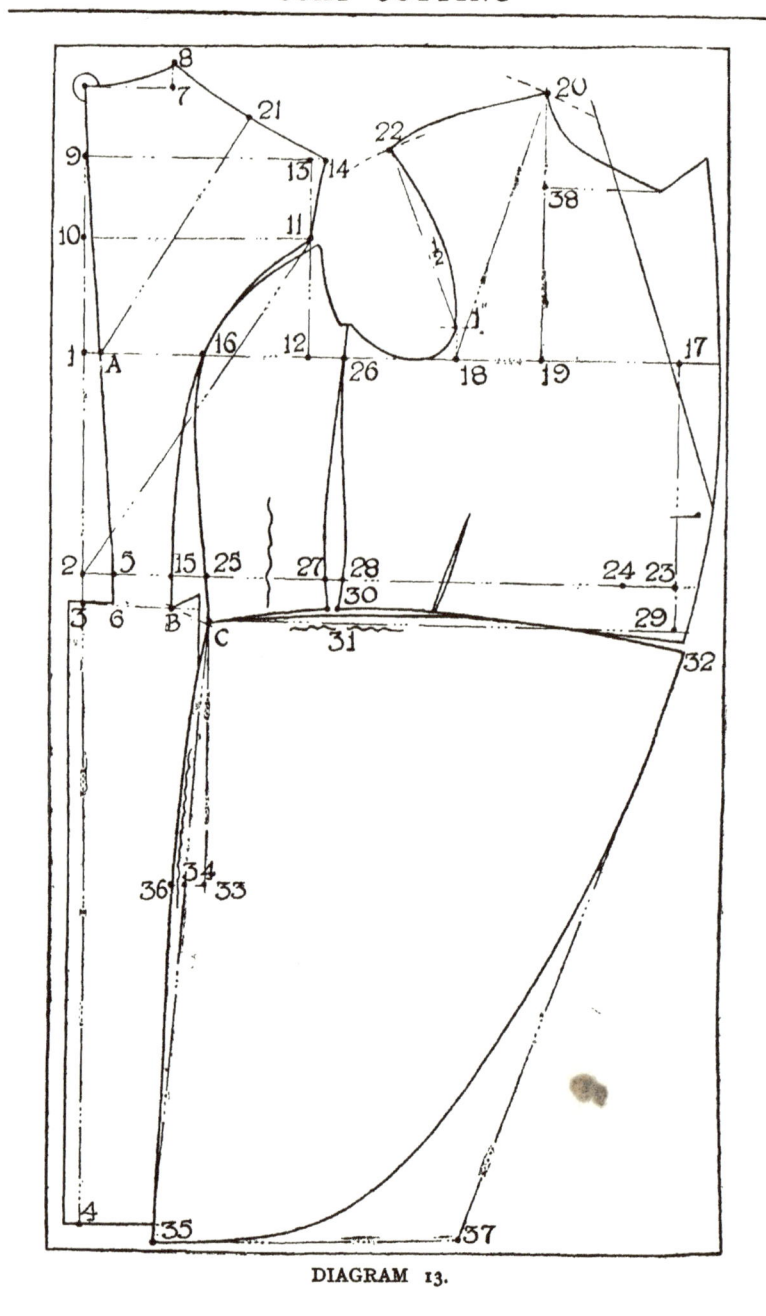

DIAGRAM 13.

COAT CUTTING

Curve the waist seam of the body part from C up to 30 ($\frac{1}{2}''$ above the line) and down $\frac{1}{4}''$ below 29 at the front.

Add $1\frac{1}{4}''$ beyond the centre line at the button hole.

When shaping the waist seam of skirt, take out $\frac{1}{4}''$ between 30 and 31, and open a similar quantity at 32.

33 from C = 9''; squared by line C - 29.

34 from 33 = 1''; the difference between the half seat and breast measures.

35 is $\frac{1}{4}''$ below line from 4 and is located by drawing through 34 from C.

Give $\frac{1}{4}''$ of round at 36 when shaping back skirt from C to 35.

37 from 35 = half 5 to 23 plus 1''.

Join 32 to 37 and curve front of skirt as shown.

38 from 20 = one-sixth scale: square out from depth of gorge. Mark out 1'' from 20 for crease line.

Take a small dart out at the waist directly below point 18. Add 1'' for pleat as shown at B and continue down to the bottom (parallel with line 3 to 4).

NOTES ON THE DRAFT

The distance 2 to 5 remains constant whatever the waist size.

For prominent blades the suppression at 15 to 25 should be increased and the underarm filled in a corresponding amount at 27.

In disproportionate waists the fronts are adjusted at 23 as in the lounge draft.

The sleeve is the same as for the lounge, point 11 representing the back pitch.

$1\frac{1}{4}''$ should be added at C to 35 when marking out on the material to form the upper half of the pleat.

When making, the side body should be strained with the iron in the waist at 27 and 25 and shrunk in the centre as shown by wavy line.

The skirt is drawn in with a thread at 31 and 36, and the resulting fullness pressed back over the hip prominence.

COAT CUTTING

DRESS COAT BY DIRECT MEASURES. Diagram 14

FEATURES :—*High and straight waist seam; three buttons; revers moderately wide and rolling to second button.*

MEASURES :—36" breast; 32" waist; 38" seat; 9" scye depth; 16½" waist length; 39" full length; 13" front shoulder; 17¾" over shoulder; 7" back width; 8" across chest. Scale 18".

INSTRUCTIONS FOR DRAFTING

THE rear section of this draft is practically the same as that for the morning coat. The fronts are curtailed at the waist to expose the white vest when the garment is in wear. If the figure is at all full-chested, a cut or dart should be taken out up the button line and an allowance made at the front. This dart can be used to advantage in keeping the lower edge of the fronts nice and snug to the figure for stout men.

The sleeve is the same as for a lounge, with slightly narrower elbow and cuff.

DRAFT

Square lines from o.
1 from o = scye depth (9);
2 from o = waist length (16½);
3 from 2 = ¾";
4 from o = full length;
Square out from all points.
5 from o = one-sixth scale plus ¼";
6 from 5 = ¼";
Shape to o;
7 from 2 = 1¼";
Square down to 8 and connect to o.
9 from 1 = one-third over-shoulder measure, plus ¾";
10 from 9 = 2¼"; square out.
11 from the inside line at 10 = back width plus ¼" (7½).
12 and 13 are located by squaring from 11.
14 from 13 = ½";
Join to 11 and shape shoulder seam to 6.
Join 11 and 2.
15 from 1 = one-ninth scale (2").
Shape blade seam giving 1" of round at 16.
17 from A = half breast plus 2¼";
18 from 17 = across chest 8";
19 from 18 = one-sixth scale (3);
Sweep the front shoulder measure less

o to 8 from 18 to locate 20 on line up from 19.
Deduct ¼" from the over-shoulder measure and apply the remainder from A to 21 and from 18 to 22 by a sweep.
22 is definitely located by applying the back shoulder width 6 to 14 less ¼" from 20.
Mark up 1" from 18 and hollow scye ½".
24 from 17 = ¾";
25 is located by squaring down from 24;
26 from 7 = half waist plus 1" (17);
27 from 15 = two-thirds 25 to 26;
28 from 12 = 1½";
29 from 27 = ¾" less than 16 to 28;
30 from 29 = one-third 25 to 26.
Mark up 1¼" above 28 for top of under-arm seam and shape to waist.
31 from 25 = 4½";
32 from 31 = 1".
B and C are found as in the morning-coat draft.
Curve the waist seam from 32 to 33 which is ½" above C line.
The skirt seam at 34 is only ¼" above C line.
Shape the front from 32 up to 35,

COAT CUTTING

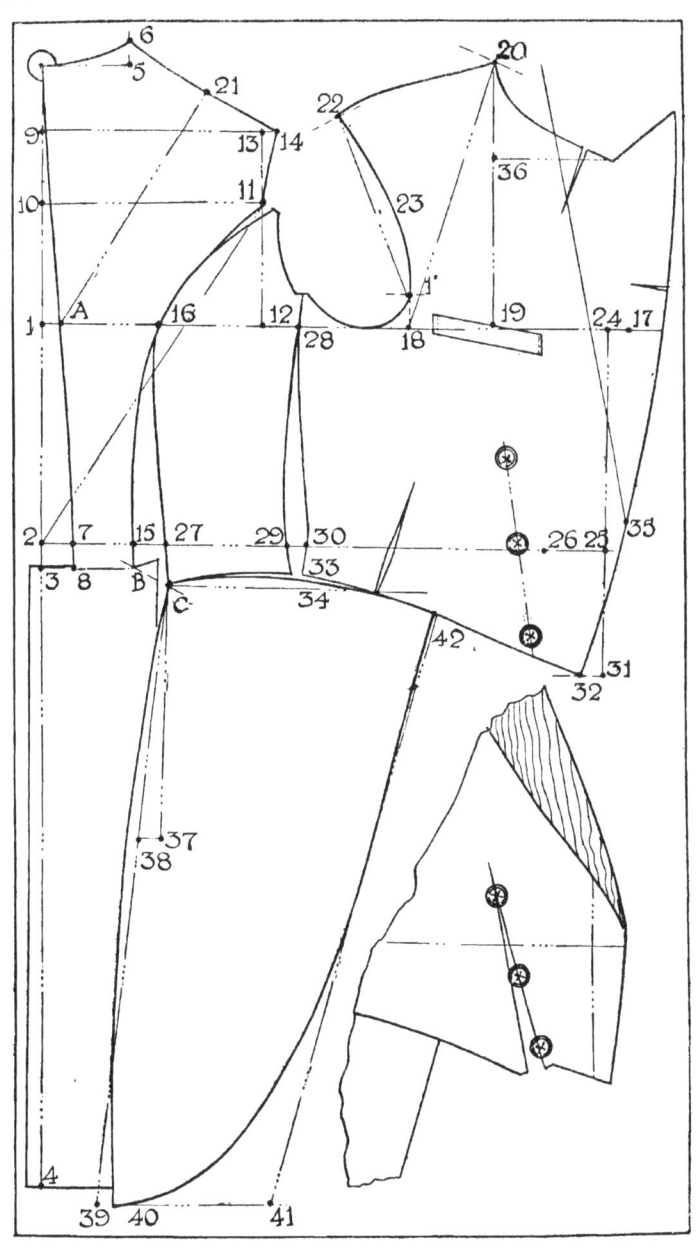

DIAGRAM 14.

COAT CUTTING

which is 1" above the waist line and ¾" out from the centre line.
36 from 20 is one-sixth scale;
Square out and shape lapel as shown. The crease line for lapel is 1" out from 20.
37 from C is 9" squared by the waist line.
38 from 37 = the difference between half breast and half hip, viz. 1".
Draw through 38 from C and extend ¼" below bottom line to 39.
40 is ½" from 39;
Curve back skirt giving ¼" of round at 38.
41 from 40 = one-eighth waist measure.
42 from 32 = one-third the forepart line from 32 to C.

Connect 42 and 41 and shape skirt as shown.

Notes on the Draft

The manipulation for this coat is the same as prescribed for the morning coat.

A beneficial effect is obtained by working a round on the crease row of the lapel. This will require an extremely short outer edge in the lapel, and to obtain this either one or two small vees may be taken out as shown in the draft.

The small diagram depicts the dart through the buttons explained above. The amount taken out depends upon the figure.

COAT CUTTING

D.B. FROCK COAT BY PROPORTION. Diagram 15

FEATURES :—*Button two, showing three; pointed lapels; silk facing; moderately high waist seam.*
MEASURES :—36" *breast;* 32" *waist;* 38" *seat;* 16½" *waist length;* 40" *full length;* 7" *half back. Scale* 18".

INSTRUCTIONS FOR DRAFTING

THIS garment, whilst not being very popular at the present time with the ordinary layman, forms the livery dress for most Nonconformist ministers. With a slight readjustment of the rever and in the number of buttons, it is also used as a general livery coat for servants employed by public bodies, banks, etc.

Compared with the morning coat, the skirt is cut much fuller in order to provide walking room. The hollowed waist seam to the skirt is responsible for the distribution of this extra width at the sides, but if this is overdone it will cause the back pleats and the fronts to gape open when the coat is being worn.

The lapel is cut separately and the front end laid to the fold of the material so that the facing is left on and a seam avoided down the edge.

DRAFT

Square lines from 0.
1 from 0 = half scale (9) ;
2 from 0 = waist length 16½" ;
3 from 2 = 1" ;
4 from 0 = full length 40 ;
Square out from the above points.
5 from 2 = 1¼" ;
6 is squared down from 5.
7 from 0 = one-sixth scale plus ¼" ;
8 from 7 = ¾" ;
9 from 0 = one-fourth 0 to 1 ;
10 from 9 = 2¾" ;
11 from the inside line at 10 = back width plus ¼".
12 and 13 are located by squaring from 11.
14 from 13 = ¼" ;
Join to 8 for shoulder seam.
Connect points 11 and 22.
15 from 5 = one-ninth scale (2) ;
Curve blade seam, giving 1" of round at 16 and continuing down from 15 to B.
17 from A = half-breast plus 2¼".

E from A = one-third half breast (6") .
18 from E = one-fourth half breast plus 2" (6½) ;
19 from 18 = one-sixth scale ;
Square up.
20 from 19 = half scale plus ¼" ;
Connect 20 and 14.
21 from 20 = 8 to 14, the back shoulder, less ¼" ;
Drop ¼".
22 from 18 = 1" ;
Join to 21 and shape scye as shown, hollowing ¼".
23 is squared down from 17.
24 from 5 = half waist plus 2" ;
25 from 15 = two-thirds waist surplus, 23 to 24 ;
26 is 1¼" from 12 ;
27 from 25 = 16 to 26 less ¾" ;
28 from 27 = one-third waist surplus, 23 to 24.
For the summit of the underarm seam mark up 1¼" from 26 and allow a seam on either side. Using 11 as a pivot, sweep B to C.
Square out from C.

COAT CUTTING

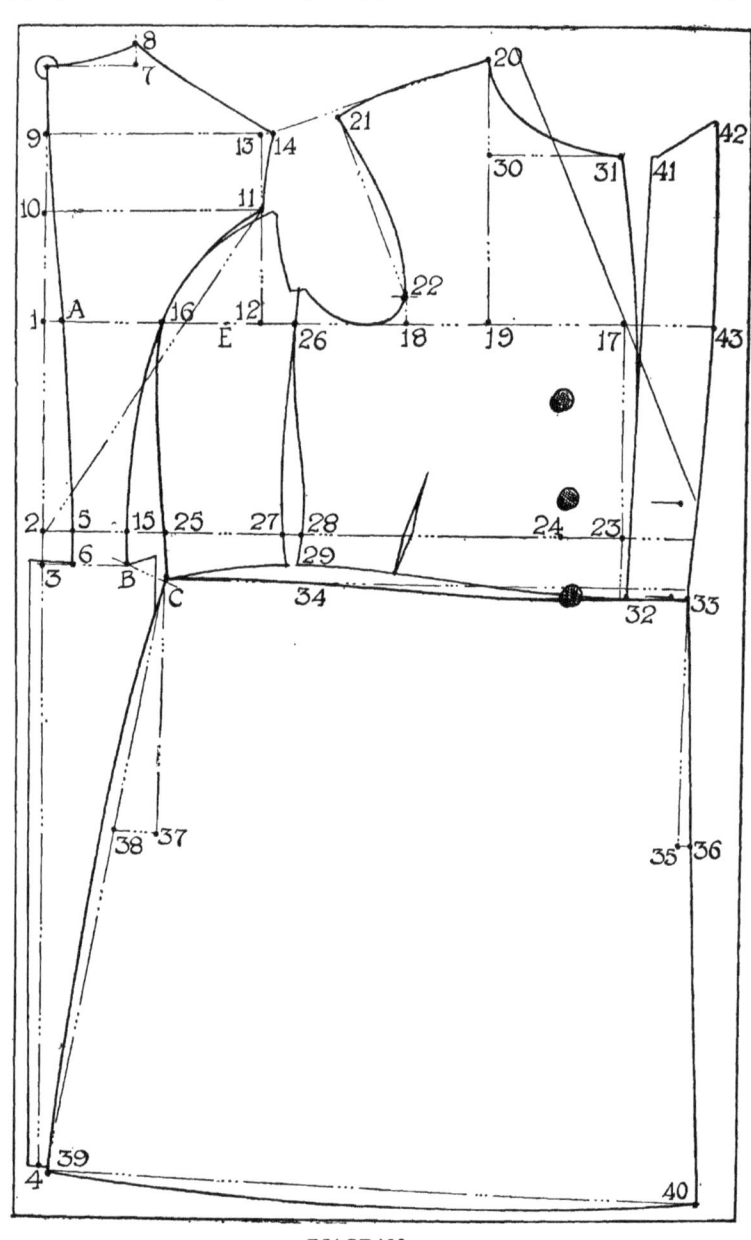

DIAGRAM 15.

COAT CUTTING

Raise waist seam of body part ¾" above C line.
30 from 20 = one-sixth scale plus ¼";
31 from 30 = 5" in this draft, but can be varied to suit lapel.
From 31 run lapel seam down to 32, allowing ¼" at 17 and 23.
32 is located ½" down from C line.
33 is 2½" out from 32.
Shape waist seam of skirt passing through C line at 34.
35 is 8½" squared down from 33.
36 from 35 = ½";
Draw through from 33.
37 is 9" from C.
38 from 37 is ½" more than half the difference between seat and breast measures.
Draw through 38 from C and down to 39.
39 from C = ¼" more than 3 to 4.
40 from 33 is ¼" more than C to 39.

41 from 31 = 1¼" curve to the body part below 17. This quantity should be reduced when a shorter rever is required.
42 from 41 = 2½".
Make the width of lapel at 43, 3".
Finish the draft by giving ¾" of round to the skirt from 39 to 40.

NOTES ON THE DRAFT

Provision for increased waist size is made on the lines prescribed for the morning coat.

No seam has been allowed down the skirt front, the facings being left "growing-on," when taking from the material.

When the waist is above normal, it is a wise policy to check up the width of top of skirt with the side-body and forepart and allow ¾" for easing-on in the region of 34.

COAT CUTTING

BACK FINISHES FOR SPORTS COATS. Diagram 16

THE fronts of Sports Coats, apart from the substitution of patches in place of the ordinary flaps, remain very much on the lines of the ordinary lounge. With the back section, however, it is different, for many features both ornamental and useful have been introduced from time to time to charm the younger generation.

The selection given here comprises the more modern ones that a cutter may be called upon to produce.

In each instance the back section is cut in the ordinary way, as for a lounge, and the adjustments made when marking out on the material, or, better still, when constructing a new back pattern.

Section A

This depicts one of the plainer finishes, frequently used in plus four suits.

Two pleats in the waist on either side of the centre may be used, or two small darts sewn out to produce a shapely waist effect.

The ordinary pattern is outlined by dot and dash lines.

4 from 3 is the amount allowed for pleat or dart at 1, and 5 to 6 for that at 2.

From 4 connect to the back neck at 7 and to the bottom of the coat.

From 6 run up to the breast line at 8 and down to the bottom of skirt.

Section B

This is rather a novel finish with a pleat extending from the shoulder seam to the waist.

A small strap emanating from the side seam covers the necessary seam at the waist.

2 is about 1¾" from shoulder end.
1 is ¾" from the side seam.
Cut the back up the pleat line 1 and 2 and open out 3" for the pleat allowance to 3 and 4.
Allow ¼" at 3 to 5 for seam.
In pleating line 4 and 3 falls under 1 and 2.

Section C

This depicts the short "knife pleat" at the side seam which is frequently used in shooting coats.

1 is 3" above the waist.
2 is at the back pitch point.
Cut the pattern up the pleat line 1 to 2 and open out 2¼" from 2 to 3 and 1¼" from 1 to 4.

Section D

Here is a very ornamental finish with shoulder yoke and waist pleats.

The back is cut across on the waist line and allowance made at 3 to 4 and 5 to 6 for the three vertical pleats.

The yoke curves from 1" to ½" above the pitch at 2.

The centre section is extended 1" to 2" for gathering as shown.

Seams must be allowed on each side of the yoke and waist seams when marking out on the material.

A half belt usually covers the waist seam.

Section E

This is one of the standard back finishes and one that has been used universally for all purposes.

A straight shoulder yoke runs across ¾" above the back pitch level, and the waist is cut across.

A "knife pleat" is introduced over the blade on line 1 to 2.

The shaded lines between 2 and 3 and 1 and 4 show the extent of the pleat (3").

This is allowed for by extending the back from 7 to 8 and 5 to 6.

COAT CUTTING

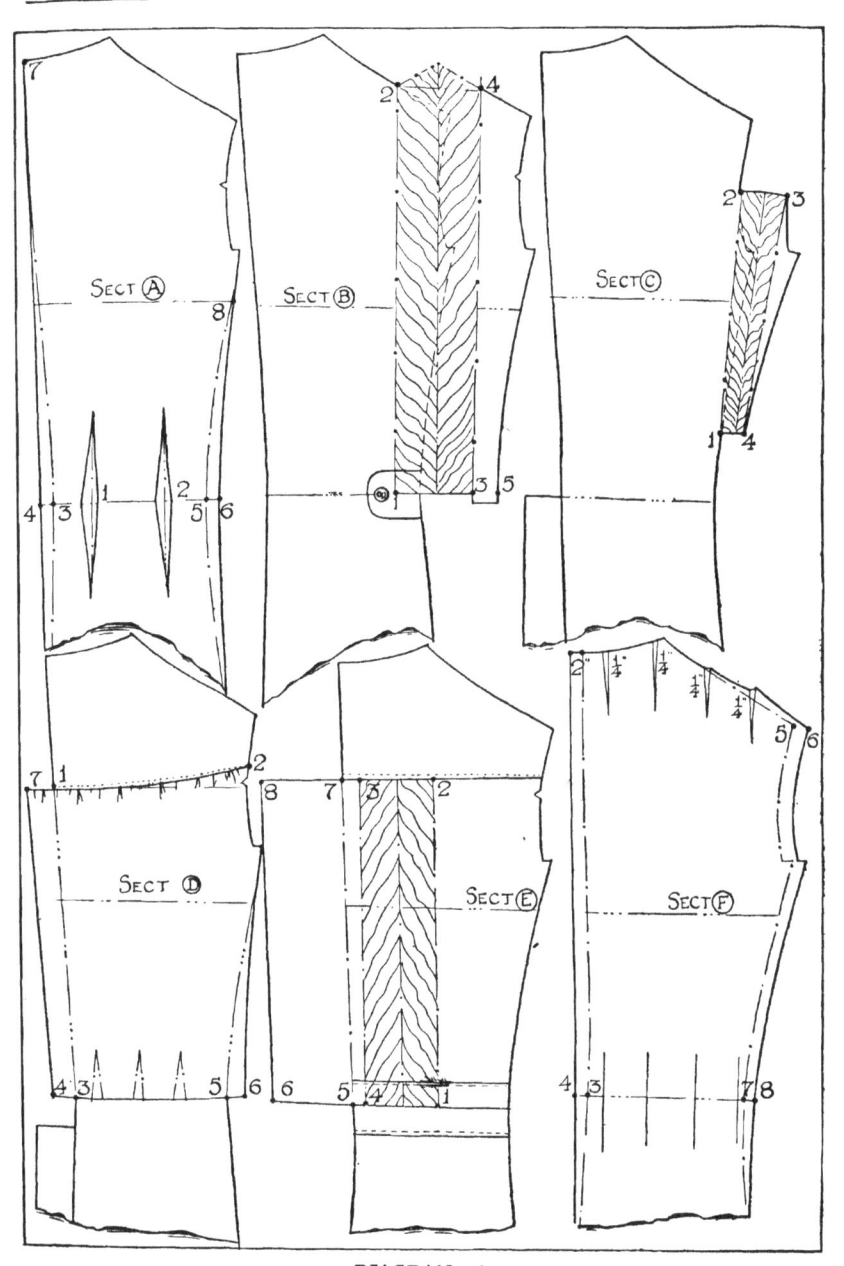

DIAGRAM 16.

COAT CUTTING

When the pleat is formed line 1 to 2 will be under line 3 to 4. Allow seams at yoke and waist.

Section F

This depicts one of the latest varieties which has as its chief virtue the distribution of extra width over the whole blade region.

Featured in a golf or shooting coat it gives a very pleasing effect.

The outline of the ordinary back is shown by dash lines.

The back is cut without a centre seam and four pin tucks or seams are run down from the neck and shoulder on either side. The same number of tucks are run through the waist.

To provide for these the centre back is extended $\frac{1}{2}''$ at 1 to 2 and 3 to 4, and the back scye side seam a similar quantity from 5 to 6 and 7 to 8.

PLATE IV

ABE MITCHELL, WEARING HIS SPECIALLY SELECTED DESIGN IN "SPORTEX."
By courtesy of Dormeuil Frères

GENTLEMEN'S GARMENT CUTTING

By PERCIVAL THICKETT

(*Author of "Defects and Remedies," "Body Coats," etc.*)

CUTTING OF OVERGARMENTS

S.B. CHESTERFIELD BY PROPORTION. Diagram 17

FEATURES :—*Single-breasted ; close-fitting waist ; centre seam and vent ; pointed lapel ; to button three.*

MEASURES :—36" *breast ;* 32" *waist ;* 38" *seat ;* 7¾" *back width ;* 16½" *waist length ;* 40" *full length.*

INSTRUCTIONS FOR DRAFTING

IT must be understood that all measures are taken as for the lounge coat, that is, the breast and waist are taken over the vest and the remainder over the jacket. The ordinary back width would be 7"; the measure given above has ⅜" added to it for the overgarment.

The scale is found by taking one-third breast plus 6", viz. one-third of 36 = 12 plus 6 = 18 scale. Below 36 breast half the measure gives the scale.

The fronts as shown are intended to be made to button through, but if a fly finish is preferred, the same method of drafting can be adhered to.

BODY PART. SECTION A

Square lines from o.
1 from o = half scale (9) ;
2 from o = waist length plus ¼" ;
3 from 2 = 2 to 1 plus 1½" ;
4 from o = full length plus making-up allowance.
5 from 2 = ¾" : 6 from 5 is the same.
Join 5 to o and curve gradually into 6 from the blades.
7 from 4 = 1¼" : join to 6 ;
8 from o = one-sixth scale plus ⅜" ;
9 from 8 = ¾" : join to o ;
10 from o = ¼th o to 1 : square out ;
11 from 10 = 2¾" : square out ;
12 from the inner line at 11 = back width plus ½" (7⅞) ;
13 and 14 are located by squaring from 12 ;
15 from 14 = ½" : join to 9 for shoulder ;
16 from 13 = 1½" ;
17 from 16 = ¾" : mark a seam each way ;
18 from 6 = width of back less 1" (6⅜) ;
19 from 3 = 2 to 18 plus ½" ;

CUTTING OF OVERGARMENTS

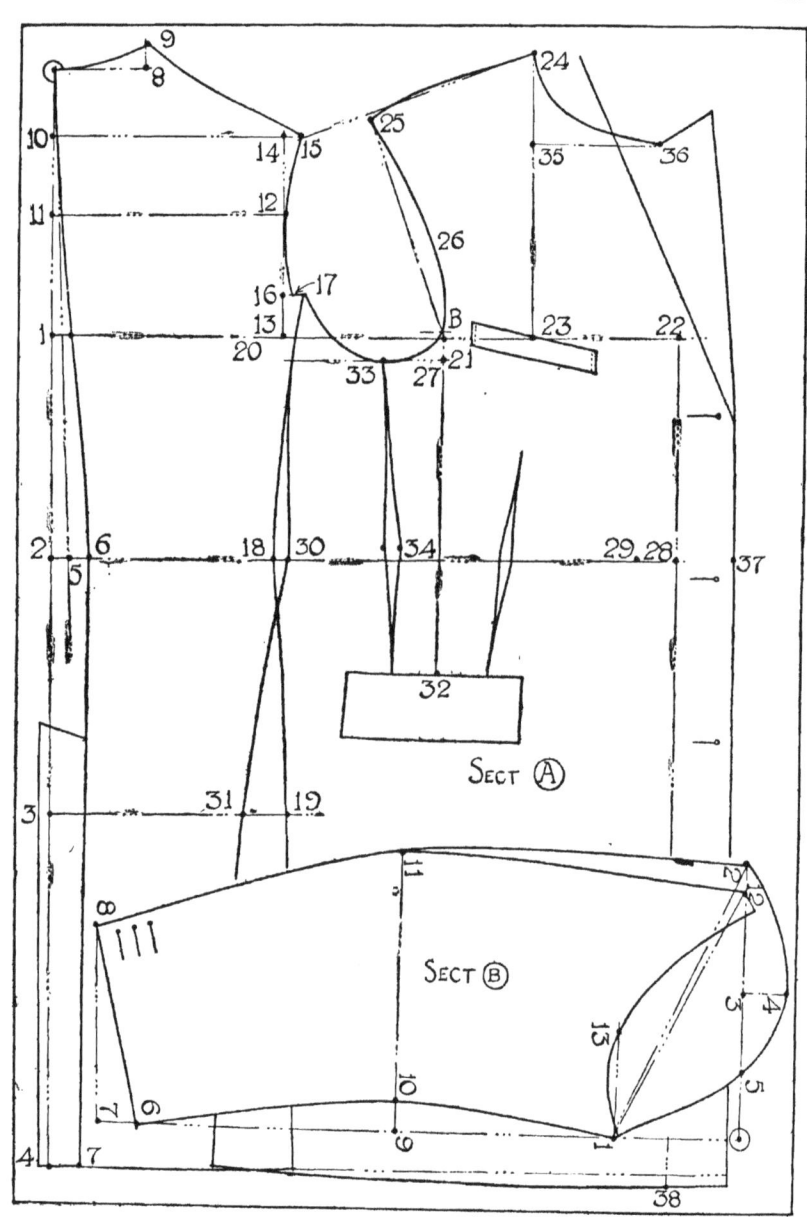

DIAGRAM 17.

CUTTING OF OVERGARMENTS

Shape side seam from 17 through 18 and 19.
20 from A = one-third of half breast (6);
21 from 20 = one-fourth of half breast plus 2¾" (7¼);
22 from A = half breast plus 3¾" (21¾);
23 from 21 = one-sixth scale plus ¼";
24 from 23 = half scale plus ½";
Join 24 and 15.
25 from 24 = 9 to 15 less ¼": drop ¼" below the line;
B from 21 = ¼": join to 25 and hollow scye ½" at 26.
27 is ¾" down from 21 for scye base: complete scye as shown.
28 is squared down from 23.
29 from 6 = half waist plus 3¾";
30 from 29 = half 28 to 29, the waist surplus;
31 from 19 = half the difference between the breast and seat measures plus ½".
Shape fore part side seam as shown from 17 through 30 and 31.
32 for centre of pocket is 11¼" down from 21 : make pocket 6½" wide.
33 from 27 = 2½";
Shape the dart to rear of pocket, suppressing at the waist 34, half the waist surplus, 28 to 29.
The breast dart running from front end of pocket towards the breast is suppressed ¼".
35 from 24 = one-sixth scale plus ¼";
Square out.
Shape neck, letting the collar end come at 36 on line from 35.
37 from 28 = 2" for button stand.
Drop foreparts ¾" at 38.
The crease line commences at 1¼" out from 24.

THE SLEEVE. SECTION B

Length of lounge sleeve = 31";
Back width 7⅜".
The preliminary preparation on the body part for the location of the pitches is similar to what was laid down for lounges. The back pitch being placed at 12 and the front one ¾" above 27 (at 21).
Square lines from o.
1 from o = 12 to 13 plus ¾";
2 direct from 1 = 12 to 15 plus 25 to 21;
3 is midway between o and 2;
4 from 3 = 12 to 15 less 1⅛";
5 is midway between o and 3;
Shape crown through 5, 4, and on to 2;
6 from 2 direct = sleeve length less back width plus 1" for overcoat (31 minus 7⅜ plus 1");
7 from 6 = 1½";
8 from 7 = one-third scale plus 1¼";
9 from 1 = half 1 to 6 less ½";
10 from 9 = 1";
Curve forearm to 1 and 6;
11 from 10 = one-third scale plus 2¾";
Shape hindarm seam to 2 and 8;
12 from 1 direct = 12 to 21, round lower half of scye;
13 from 1 = half 13 to 21, the width of scye.
Shape undersleeve, dropping ¼" below line 1 and 13.

NOTES ON THE DRAFT

If an easier-fitting waist is required, the front dart can be omitted, and, in heavy materials, the underarm dart also.
Where a full skirt is desired, and at the same time a shaped waist, extend point 31 a further ½" to 1".
No wadding has been provided for in the shoulders. Where it is essential that the shoulders should be built up raise the scye end at 25 and allow a little on the sleeve crown at 4.
A wider or narrower shoulder effect should be regulated after the completion of the ordinary draft. This will automatically increase or decrease the height of the shoulder ends to agree with the position of the scye seam on the body.

CUTTING OF OVERGARMENTS

SAC CHESTERFIELD. BY DIRECT MEASURES. Diagram 18

FEATURES :—*Single-breasted; step lapel; loose-fitting, with draped back; patch or slit pockets; seam and vent in back.*
MEASURES :—36" breast; 32" waist; 9" scye depth; 16½" waist length; 40" full length; 13¾" front shoulder; 17¾" over shoulder; 8⅜" across chest; 7⅜" across back. Scale 18".

INSTRUCTIONS FOR DRAFTING

THE above direct measures are taken as for the lounge coat and carry the following additions for the overgarment: —Front shoulder ⅜"; across chest ⅜"; back width ⅜".

If the draft is required by proportion the system laid down for the Close-fitting Chesterfield can be used, without alteration to width and height quantities.

If the back is required without a centre seam, the material for the back should be cut out on the large size, then shrunk over the blade to the shape of the pattern.

The sleeve for this coat will be drafted as described for the ordinary Chesterfield, but due attention must be paid to the overlap at the side seam (25 to 27) when measuring round the scye for the undersleeve.

DRAFT

Square lines from 0.
1 from 0 = scye depth (9");
2 from 0 = waist length plus ¼";
3 from 0 = full length (40");
4 from 1 = one-third over-shoulder measure plus ⅜": square out.
5 from 4 = 2¼": square out;
6 from 2 = ⅜";
To locate 7, draw through 6 starting at point 5.
Round the back centre gradually from A to 0.
8 from 0 = one-sixth scale plus ⅜";
9 from 8 = ¼": join to 0;
10 from the inner line at 5 = back width plus ¼" (7⅞);
11 and 12 are located by squaring from 10;
13 from 12 = ¼": join to 9 for shoulder seam;
14 from A = half breast plus 3¾" (21¾);
15 from 14 = across chest measure 8⅜";

16 from 15 = one-sixth scale plus ¼": square up.
Apply the front shoulder measure less 0 to 8 from 15 by sweep to 17.
Apply the over-shoulder measure less ¼" from A to 18 and then by sweep from 15 to 19.
19 is definitely located by applying the back shoulder width 9 to 13 less ¼" from 17.
20 is ¼" above 15: join to 19.
Hollow scye ¼" at 21.
22 from 15 = ¾" for scye base;
Square across.
23 from 11 = one-third the scye width 11 to 15.
24 is located by squaring down from 23.
25 is ¼" out from line 23 and is situated midway between the breast line and the base of scye.
26 from 24 = 1¼": draw through from 25;
27 from 23 line = ¼" and is in line with point 25;
28 from 24 = 1¼": draw through from 27;

CUTTING OF OVERGARMENTS

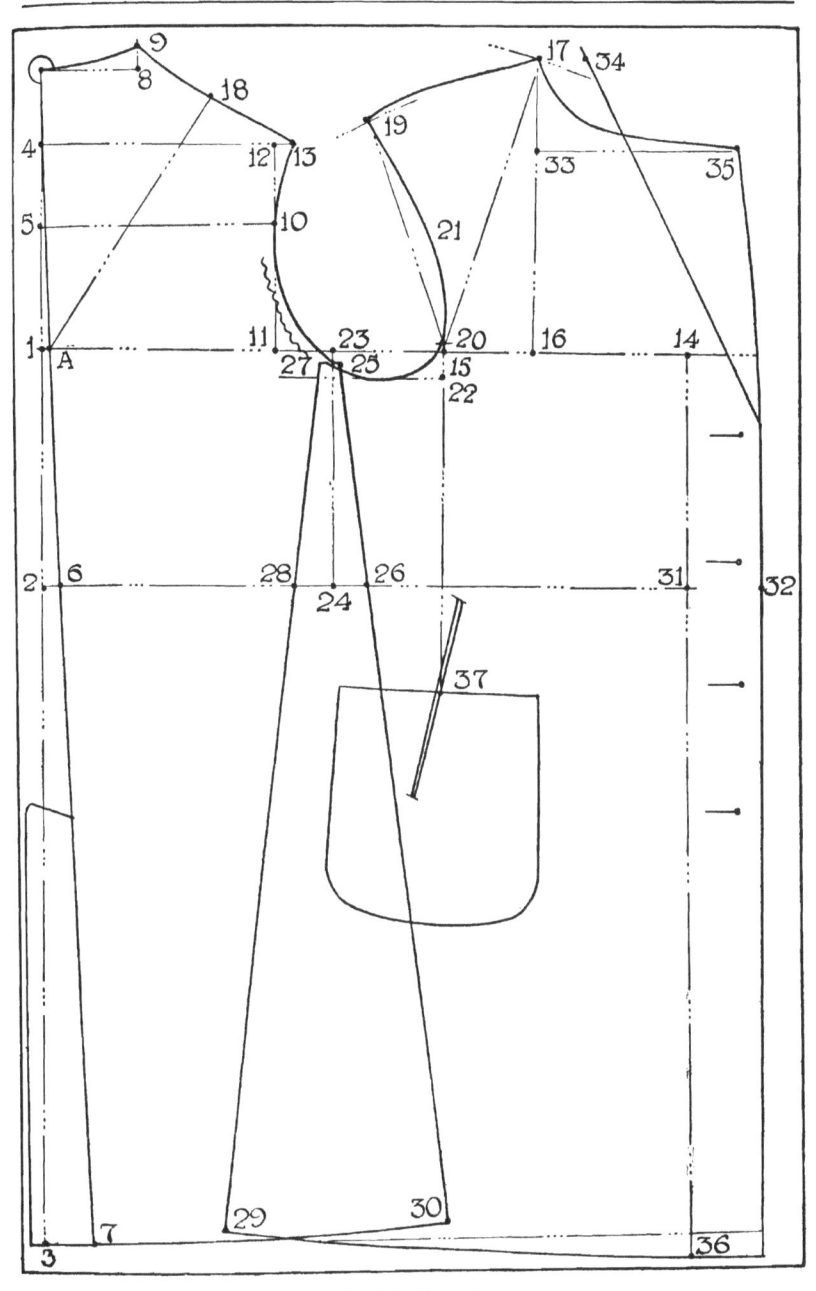

DIAGRAM 18.

CUTTING OF OVERGARMENTS

29 from 23 = A to 7;
30 from 23 is the same.
31 is squared down from 14.
32 from 31 = 2" for front edge.
33 from 17 = one-sixth scale (3");
Square out.
34 for crease line is 1¼" out from 17.
35 is on line from 33 and forms the guiding point for the shape of the neck. The distance out from crease line depends on the width of lapel required.
Extend the bottom of forepart ¾" below the bottom construction line at 36 and join to 29.
Join 7 to 30 for base of back-part.
The centre of pocket at 37 is found by squaring 11½" down from 15.

NOTES ON THE DRAFT

In order to ensure a well-draped back scye, the back must either be drawn in well or shrunk in the region of the wavy line.

The amount of skirt given in the draft will be found suitable for average purposes, but if more is desired, points 27 and 28 should be extended further from line 23-24.

There is no fixed position for the vent, the depth being regulated to accord with the prevailing fashion, but for a safe guide, at the present time one-third the full length plus 2" up from the bottom should be sufficient.

PLEATED BACK CHESTERFIELD. Diagram 19

FEATURES :—*Double-breasted, buttoning two ; centre seam with box pleat from waist ; side pleats ; half belt.*

MEASURES :—36″ *breast ;* 32″ *waist ;* 38″ *seat ;* 9″ *scye depth ;* 16½″ *waist length ;* 40″ *full length ;* 13⅜″ *front shoulder ;* 17¾″ *over shoulder ;* 7⅜″ *across back ;* 8⅜″ *across chest. Scale* 18″.

INSTRUCTIONS FOR DRAFTING

WITH the ordinary back as given with the close-fitting style, this draft can be used for a semi-fitting model.

The allowance for the quantity taken up in the knife pleat under the belt is allowed on either side of the ordinary back outline.

Additions have already been made to the Direct Measures to allow for the overgarment. (See Sac Chesterfield draft.)

DRAFT

Square lines from 0.
1 from 0 = scye depth (9″) ;
2 from 0 = waist length plus ¼″ ;
3 from 2 = 1 to 2 plus 1½″ ;
4 from 0 = full length (40″) ;
5 from 2 = ¾″ : join to 0.
6 from 5 = ¾″ : curve gradually into the above line.
7 is squared down from 5 by waist line and forms the centre back line.
8 from 0 = one-sixth scale plus ⅜″ ;
9 from 8 = ¾″ : connect to 0 for back neck ;
10 from 1 = one-third the over-shoulder measure, plus ¾″ : square out ;
11 from 10 = 2¾″ : square out ;
12 from 11 (inner line) = back width plus ½″ ;
13 and 14 are located by squaring up and down from 12 ;
15 from 14 = ½″ : join to 9 for shoulder seam ;
16 from 13 = 1¼″ : square out ;
17 from 16 for top of side seam = 1″ ;
Mark a seam on either side.
18 from 6 = back width less 1″ (6⅜″) ;
19 from 18 = two-thirds of the amount taken up by the pleat, 1½″ : the remaining third for pleat is given at 6 to 5 ;
20 from 3 = 2 to 18 plus ½″ ;
21 from 20 = 18 to 19 ;
Shape side seam of back through 19 and 21 ;
22 from A = half breast plus 3¾″ ;
23 from 22 = across chest 8⅜″ ;
24 from 23 = one-sixth scale, plus ¼″.
Sweep the front shoulder measure, less back neck (0 to 8) from 23 to 25.
Deduct ½″ from the over-shoulder measure and apply the remainder from A to 26 and then by sweep from 23 to 27.
27 is definitely located by applying the back shoulder width, 9 to 15, less ¼″ from 25.
28 is ¼″ above 23 ;
Join to 27 and hollow ½″ ;
29 is ¾″ down from 23 ;
Square across for base of scye ;
30 is squared down from 22 ;
31 from 6 = half waist plus 3¾″ ;
32 from 18 = half the waist surplus shown from 30 to 31 ;
33 from 20 = half the difference between the breast and seat measures plus ½″ ;
Shape side seam from 17.
34 for centre of pocket is 11½″ down from 23 ;
35 is 2½″ from 29 ;
Shape underarm dart to a point ½″ in the rear of pocket and suppress the waist half the waist surplus (30 to 31) at 36 ;

CUTTING OF OVERGARMENTS

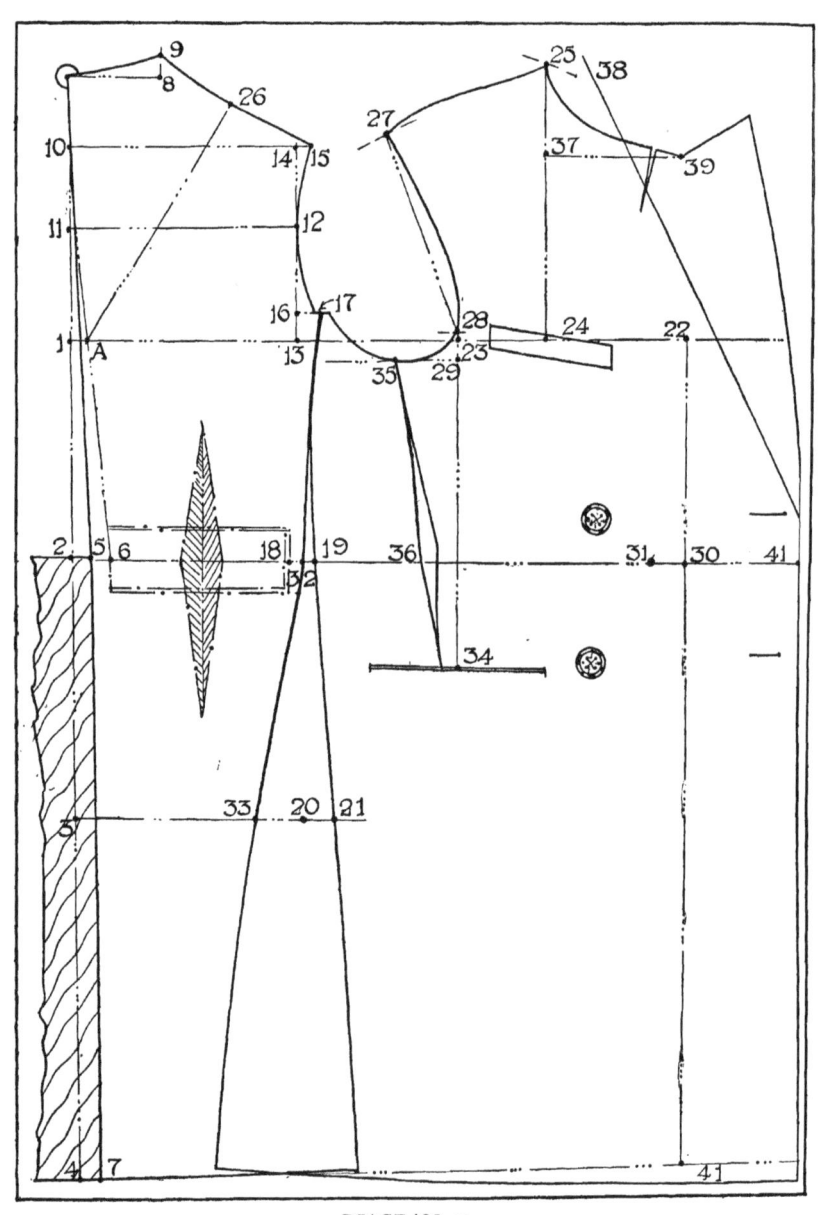

DIAGRAM 19.

CUTTING OF OVERGARMENTS

37 from 25 = one-sixth scale plus $\tfrac{1}{4}''$: square out.
38 from 25 for crease line is $1\tfrac{1}{4}''$;
41 from 30 = $4''$ to $4\tfrac{1}{2}''$ for the front overlap.
Arrange the position of first buttonhole $1\tfrac{1}{2}''$ above the waist and draw crease row from 38.
39 is squared out from 37.
Shape neck as shown and take a small vee out.
Give $\tfrac{3}{4}''$ below bottom construction line at 41 and complete draft.

Notes on the Draft

The length of the half belt is shown on the draft and extends the width of normal back from 6 to 18.
When the material is thick and clumsy the dart at 35 can be run out a little below the breast line. This would have the effect of giving ease in the scye region.
The allowance for the back pleat from 5 should be not less than $4''$ and not less than $6''$ at the base from 7.

CUTTING OF OVERGARMENTS

RAGLAN OVERCOAT. Diagram 20

FEATURES :—*Single-breasted ; pointed lapel ; very loose-fitting ; draped back scye ; three-piece sleeve.*
MEASURES :—36" *breast ;* 32" *waist ;* 16½" *waist length ;* 40" *full length ;* 7⅜" *back width.* Scale 18".

INSTRUCTIONS FOR DRAFTING

THIS draft is based on the Proportionate System, but where Direct Measures have been taken they can be applied as laid down in previous drafts.

The Raglan effect in the body part is obtained by cutting away the shoulder section of the ordinary sac coat. The amount of curve given to the diagonal seams is purely a matter of taste, but care must be taken to see that they enter the scye at the back and front sleeve pitches.

BODY PART. SECTION A

Square lines from 0.
1 from 0 = half scale ;
2 from 0 = waist length plus ¼" ;
3 from 0 = full length ;
4 from 0 = one-fourth 0 to 1 ;
5 from 4 = 2¾" ;
6 from 2 = ¾" ;
Draw through 6 from 5, thus locating 7 on bottom line ;
8 from 5 = back width plus ¼" ;
10 and 9 are located by squaring up and down from 8 ;
11 from 10 = ½" ;
12 from 0 = one-sixth scale plus ⅜" ;
13 from 12 = ¾" : join to 0 ;
14 from A = one-third of half breast (6") ;
15 from 14 = one-fourth half breast plus 2¼" ;
16 from A = half breast plus 3¾" ;
17 from 15 = one-sixth scale plus ¼" : square up ;
18 from 17 = half scale plus ½" ; Join to 11 ;
19 from 18 = ¼" less than 11 to 13 ;
20 is ¼" above 15 ;
21 from 15 is 1" down ;
Square across for base of scye ;
22 is midway between 9 and 15, but can be varied to suit the laying-out on the material.
B is squared from 22 ;

23 from 22 = ¼" ;
24 from 22 = ½" ;
25 and 26 are each 1¼" out from B.
Draw through 26 from 23 and 25 from 24 ;
C and D are located on the base line from 21 ;
27 from 18 = one-sixth scale plus ¼" ;
Square out and shape lapel.

ADJUSTMENT FOR RAGLAN EFFECT

28 from 18 = ½" ;
Join to 15 by a graceful curve ;
29 from 8 = ¼" : curve from 13 through this point and into scye at W ;
W is 1½" down from 8 ;
The front pitch of the sleeve is located on the breast line.

SLEEVE. SECTION B

Square lines from 0.
1 from 0 = 8 to 9 plus ¾" ;
2 from 1 direct = 8 to 11 plus 19 to 15 ;
3 from 0 = 8 to 11 less 1¼" ;
Square out ;
5 from 1 direct = 15 to 19 less ¼" ;
6 from 2 direct = 8 to 11 plus 1¼" ;
4 is on line from 1 and from 2 = the amount 8 to 29.
Take the distance on the straight line from 15 to 28 and sweep this from 1 to 7.

CUTTING OF OVERGARMENTS

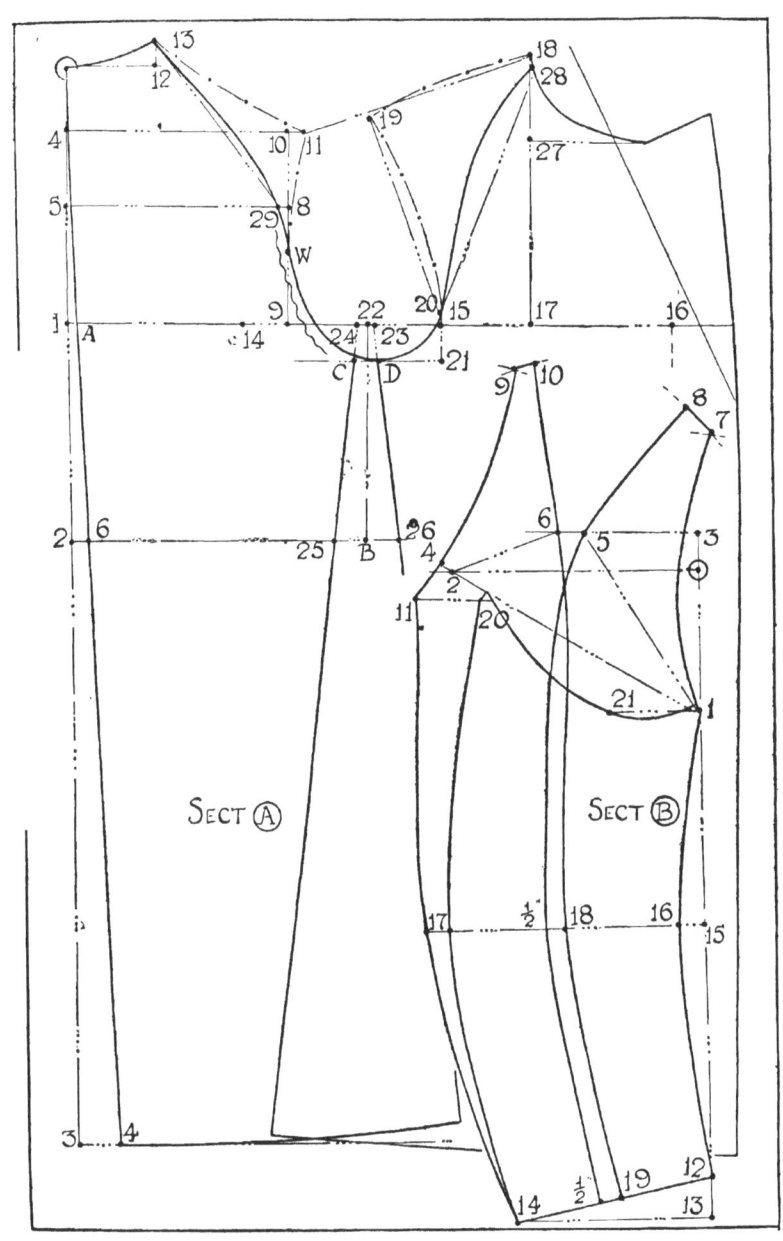

DIAGRAM 20.

CUTTING OF OVERGARMENTS

Take the distance 29 to 13 and sweep this from 4 towards 9.
Take the distance 13 to 11, less ¼", and sweep from 5 definitely to locate 7.
Using the same quantity (11 to 13 minus ¼) sweep from 6 to locate point 9.
7 to 8 on sweep from 5 = 1", comprising ½" for seams and ½" lost at 18 to 28;
9 to 10 on sweep from 5 = ½" for two seams.
Curve from 7 to 1 to compare with 28 to 15.
Curve from 9 to 4 to compare with 13 to 29 and continue down to 11, 1½" or the amount the pitch has been dropped from 29 to W.
12 from 2 = the sleeve length less back width (7⅜) and plus 1" for the overgarment.
13 from 12 = 1½": square out;
14 from 12 = one-third scale plus 1½";
15 from 1 = half 1 to 12 less ½";
16 from 15 = 1";
17 from 16 = one-third scale plus 3¼";
18 from 16 = half the distance to 17 less ¼";
19 from 12 = half the distance to 14 less ¼".
Curve back half of sleeve from 10 through 5, 18, and 19.
Curve the front part of the sleeve from 8 through 5 and on to the bottom, allowing ½" for seams beyond 18 and 19.
21 from 1 = half the width of scye (9 to 15) plus ½";
20 direct from 1 = W to D plus C to 15, the lower half of the scye;
Shape the undersleeve coming inside point 17, ¾".

Notes on the Draft

No adjustment must be made to the sleeve draft to accommodate irregularities in form or attitude. These must be embodied in the coat draft before the sleeve is constructed.

This sleeve is arranged to give a natural shoulder-width effect, but if a fuller and wider top part is desired, this can be obtained by overlapping the centre a little more below points 5 and 6.

The back should be drawn in, in the region of the wavy line at back scye.

CUTTING OF OVERGARMENTS

VARIETIES OF RAGLAN SLEEVES. Diagram 21

THIS diagram demonstrates how the one and two-piece Raglan sleeves are constructed. The former is used mostly for slip-on coats in rainproof materials and requires very careful treatment in order to procure a graceful hang.

The two-piece is a much more elegant sleeve and can be used for almost any purpose.

The ordinary sac coat is drafted as for the three-piece sleeve and the scye deepened.

BODY PART. SECTION A

For a Prussian collar finish the neck is carried forward $\frac{1}{2}''$ as shown from A to B. This adjustment is also essential in coats that are cut extremely deep in the scye.
B to C = one-sixth scale plus $\frac{1}{4}''$;
D from C = one-sixth scale plus $\frac{1}{2}''$;
Curve neck as shown.
The buttonhole side extends 1" beyond the centre line to E and the button side 2" to F.
Points 1 up to 7 remain as in the previous draft.
8 from 3 = half 3 to 9 less $\frac{1}{2}''$.
Shape the scye, dropping 2" or more below the breast line at 10 and 11.

TWO-PIECE SLEEVE. SECTION B

Square lines from 0.
1 from 0 = 1 to 9 of scye plus $\frac{1}{2}''$;
2 from 1 direct = 1 to 6 and 3 to 17;
3 from 0 = 1 to 6 less $1\frac{1}{2}''$;
4 from 1 = 3 to 17 less $\frac{1}{4}''$;
5 from 2 = 1 to 6 plus $1\frac{1}{4}''$.
Take the distance on the straight line from 3 to 5 and sweep this from 1 to 6.
Take the distance 2 to 1 and sweep this from 2 to 7.
Take the distance 2 to 6 less $\frac{1}{4}''$ and sweep this from 4 to locate definitely point 6 of sleeve.
Using the same quantity sweep from 5 to locate definitely point 7.
6 to 8 on sweep = 1";
7 to 9 = $\frac{1}{2}''$;
10 from 1 = half the distance 8 to 11;
11 from 10 squared out = 6" always;
12 from 11 = $\frac{1}{4}''$: draw through 10;
13 from 1 = 3 to 10 of scye;
14 from 2 = 1 round to 11 of scye.
15 is midway between 13 and 14;
16 is squared down from 15 and from 2 = the sleeve length less back width.
Square out on either side of 16.
17 and 18 are one-third scale plus $\frac{1}{2}''$ from 16 for width of cuff.
When shaping from 17 to 18, give a little round between 16 and 18 and hollow above line 16 to 17.
Shape back part of sleeve from 9 through 5 and down to 16.
Shape front part from 8 through 4 and down to 16, overlapping $\frac{3}{4}''$ at 15 and $\frac{1}{2}''$ at the cuff.
Curve 6 to 1 to agree with forepart shoulder and continue down to 13.
Join 7 and 2 and continue down to 14.

ONE-PIECE SLEEVE. SECTION B
(Dot and dash lines.)

This sleeve below points 1 and 14 is the same as the two-piece, excepting, of course, that there is no centre seam.
To form the single horn of the sleeve, take the distance 3 to 5, add $\frac{3}{4}''$ for fullness and sweep from 1 towards A.
Take the distance 1 to 2, add $\frac{3}{4}''$ and sweep from 2 towards A.
A is definitely located where the two sweeps above intersect.
Mark out $\frac{1}{2}''$ on either side of A as shown at B and C.
Connect B to 2 and C to 1.
The lower part of the sleeve continues from 1 to 13 and 2 to 14. The

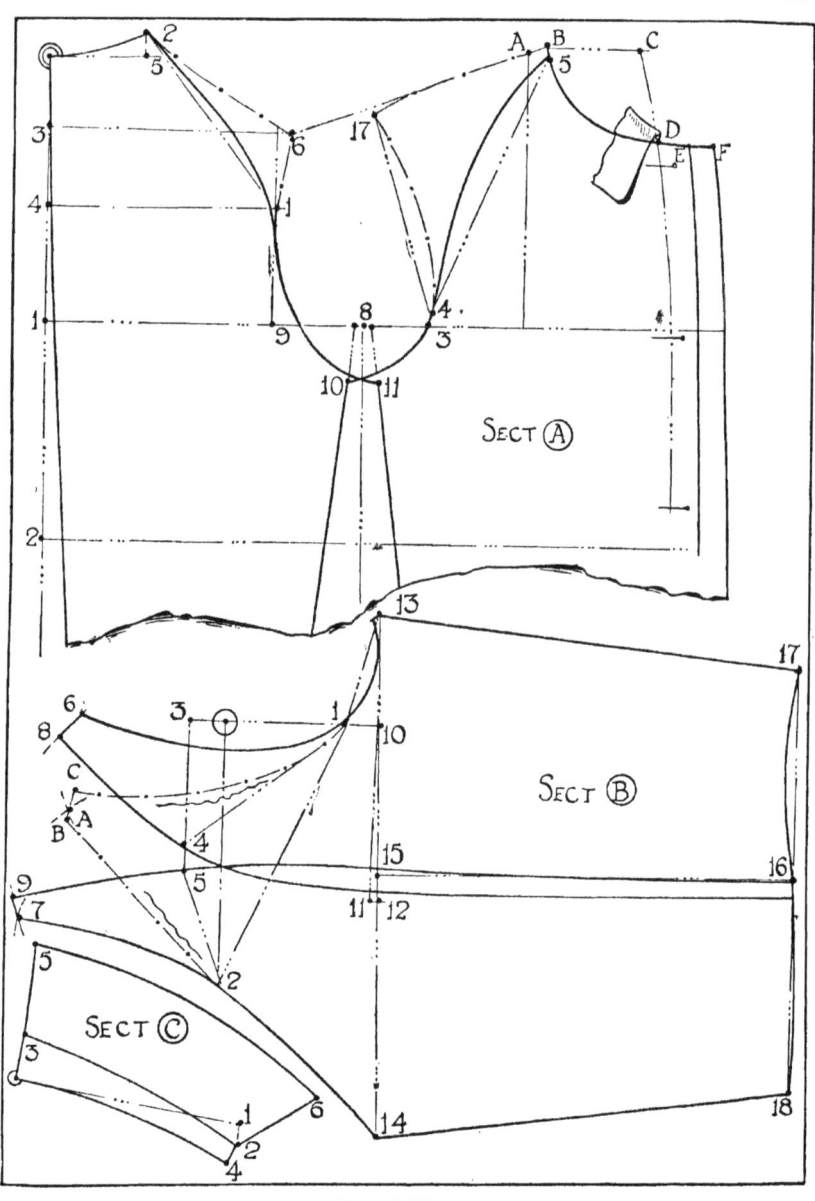

CUTTING OF OVERGARMENTS

DIAGRAM 21.

CUTTING OF OVERGARMENTS

sleeve fullness is introduced in the region of the wavy line.

PRUSSIAN COLLAR. SECTION C

Square lines from 0.
1 from 0 = 0 to 2 and B round to D less $\frac{1}{2}''$.

2 from 1 = $\frac{3}{4}''$;
3 from 0 = $1\frac{1}{2}''$, the "stand";
4 from 2 = $\frac{3}{4}''$;
5 from 0 = $3\frac{1}{2}''$;

Shape the front end of collar, making the distance from 2 to 6, $\frac{1}{2}''$ more than the back.

CUTTING OF OVERGARMENTS

SPLIT-SLEEVED CHESTERFIELD. Diagram 22

FEATURES :—*Single-breasted ; loose-fitting ; single-breasted lapel ; slit pockets ; three-piece sleeve.*
MEASURES :—36" *breast ;* 32" *waist ;* 38" *seat ;* 7⅜" *back width ;* 16½" *waist length ;* 40" *full length. Scale* 18".

INSTRUCTIONS FOR DRAFTING

IN order to connect with the centre seam of the sleeve, the shoulder seam is moved to the summit of the shoulder. This entails an addition of 1" on the back part and a corresponding reduction at the forepart shoulder end.

The underarm seam of body part can be moved nearer the centre of the scye, if it will help when taking the pattern from the material.

The sleeve heads of these coats are usually stitched over, so an inlay will be required round the sleeve crown.

BODY PART. SECTION A

Square lines from 0.
1 from 0 = half scale (9) ;
2 from 0 = waist length (16½) ;
3 from 0 = one-fourth 0 to 1 ;
4 from 3 = 2¾" ;
5 from 2 = ¾" ;
Draw through from 4 and curve back up to 0 ;
6 from 0 = one-sixth scale plus ⅜" (3⅜) ;
7 from 6 = ¾" ;
8 from 4 = back width plus ½" ;
9 and 10 are found by squaring from 8 ;
11 from 10 = ½" ;
Join to 7 ;
12 from A = one-third of half breast measure ;
13 from 12 = one-fourth of half breast plus 2¾" ;
14 from A = half breast plus 3¾" ;
15 from 13 = one-sixth scale plus ¼" ;
16 from 15 = half scale plus ¼" ;
Connect 16 and 11.
17 from 16 = 7 to 11 less ¼" ;
Mark up ¼" from 13 and join to 17 ;
18 is 1" from 13 ;
19 from 9 = one-third the distance across scye from 9 to 13.
20 is squared down from 19.
21 and 22 are each 1¼" from 20.

23 is ¼" from line 19.
24 is ½" from line 19.
Shape scye and side seam as shown.
B is squared down from 14.
C is one-sixth scale plus ¼" from 16 ; square out.
Add 2" on the front beyond B line.
26 is found by continuing the back scye 1" above 11 ;
Join to 7.
25 is 1" down from 17.
T is ¾" above 18.
W is 1½" below 8.
The top of pocket is 9" down from 13.

THE SLEEVE. SECTION B

Square lines from 0.
1 from 0 = 8 to 9 plus ¾" ;
2 direct from 1 = 8 to 26 plus 25 to T ;
3 from 0 = 1¼" less than 8 to 11 : square out.
Take the distance from T to 25 plus ¼" and apply from 1 to locate point 4 on top line ;
Take the distance 8 to 26 plus ½" and apply from 2 to 5 ;
Connect 1 to 4, giving 1" of round and 5 to 2, giving ½" of round ;
Continue the sleeve crown 1½" from 2 to 6 ;

CUTTING OF OVERGARMENTS

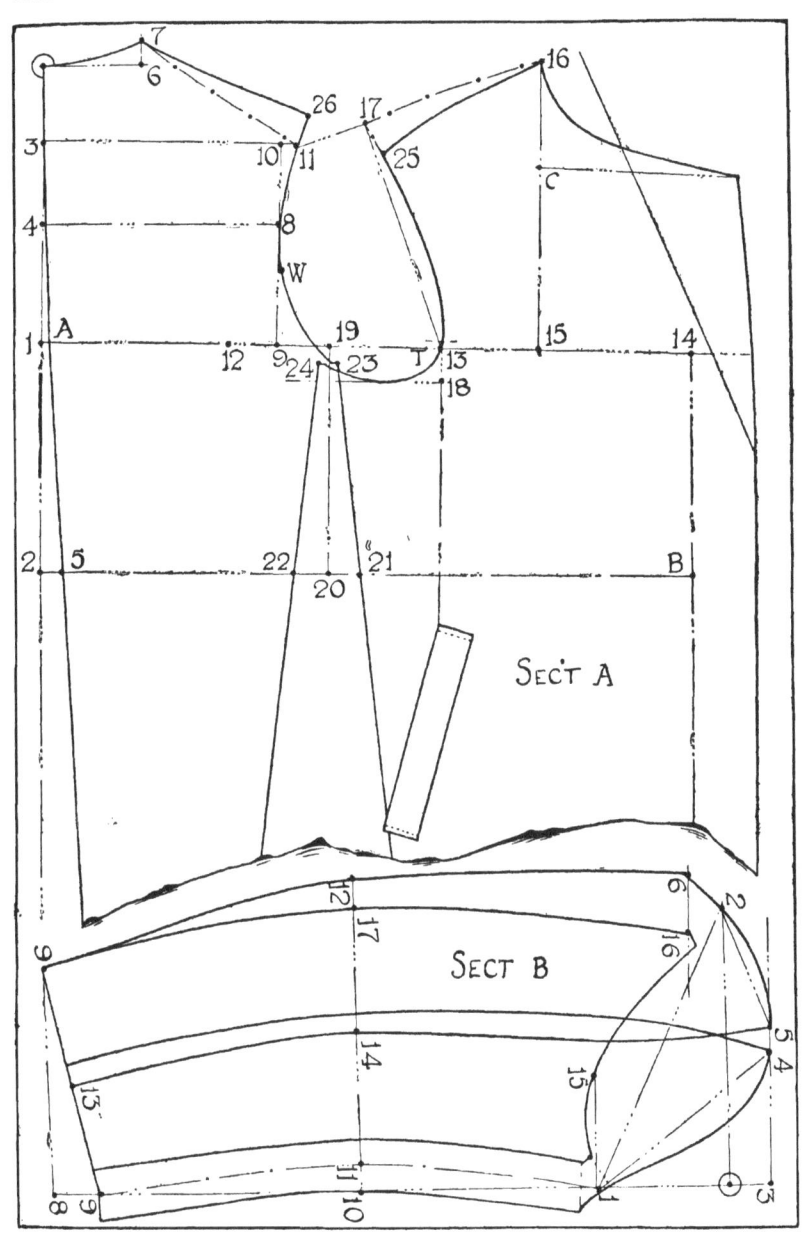

DIAGRAM 22.

CUTTING OF OVERGARMENTS

7 from 2 direct is the sleeve length plus 1″ and less the back width 7⅜″;
8 from 7 = 1½″: square out;
9 from 7 = one-third scale plus 1¼″;
10 from 1 = half 1 to 7 less ¼″; Square out;
11 from 10 = 1″;
12 from 10 = one-third scale plus 3¼″;
13 from 7 = half 7 to 9 less ¼″;
14 from 11 = half 11 to 12;
15 from 1 = half scye width 9 to 13 plus ½″;
16 from 1 direct = W to 23 plus 24 to T;
17 from 12 = ¾″.

Complete draft by joining 5, 14, and 13, and allowing ¼″ for seams when drawing from 4 to cuff.
Alter for false fore-arm as described in article on Sleeve Construction.

Notes on the Draft

When sewing in the sleeve, see that the hindarm seam at 6 joins back scye at W.
The back scye requires nicely drawing-in, in order to obtain a straight and clean hang to the skirt at the sides.

GENTLEMEN'S GARMENT CUTTING

By PERCIVAL THICKETT

(*Author of "Defects and Remedies," "Body Coats," etc.*)

CUTTING FOR CORPULENT FIGURES

LOUNGE JACKET. Diagram 23

FEATURES :—*Single-breasted ; button two ; pointed lapels ; close-fitting waist ; centre seam ; no vent.*

MEASURES :—48" breast ; 52" waist ; 51" seat ; 11" scye depth ; 18¼" waist length ; 31" full length ; 16" front shoulder ; 22" over shoulder ; 10¼" across chest ; 9" across back. Scale 22".

FORMULA FOR ASCERTAINING AMOUNT OF DISPROPORTION

IN order to distribute correctly the waist increment in the draft, it is essential to know the amount of disproportion ; in other words, the amount the waist is above the proportionate size. This is found as follows :—Deduct 4" from the measured breast to find the proportionate waist ; compare the result with the actual waist measured on the figure and the difference will register the amount of disproportion, i.e. 48 breast less 4" = 44 P.W. 52 actual waist minus 44 P.W. gives 8" disproportion.

INSTRUCTIONS FOR DRAFTING

No alteration is required in the method of finding the scale for corpulent figures. Apart from the slight alteration shown at 20 to 22, no change is necessary in drafting by the proportionate system previously described.

The " belly cut " described in the instructions below should not be included for any figure that does not show a waist measure larger than the breast size.

BODY PART. SECTION A

Disproportion 8".
Square lines from o.
1 from o = scye depth 11" ;
2 from o = waist length 18¼" ;
3 from 2 = 1 to 2 plus 1½" ;
4 from o = full length ;
5 from 2 = ¼" : join to o ;
6 from 5 = ½" ;
Curve gradually to line 5 ;
7 from 4 = 6 from 2 ;

CUTTING FOR CORPULENT FIGURES

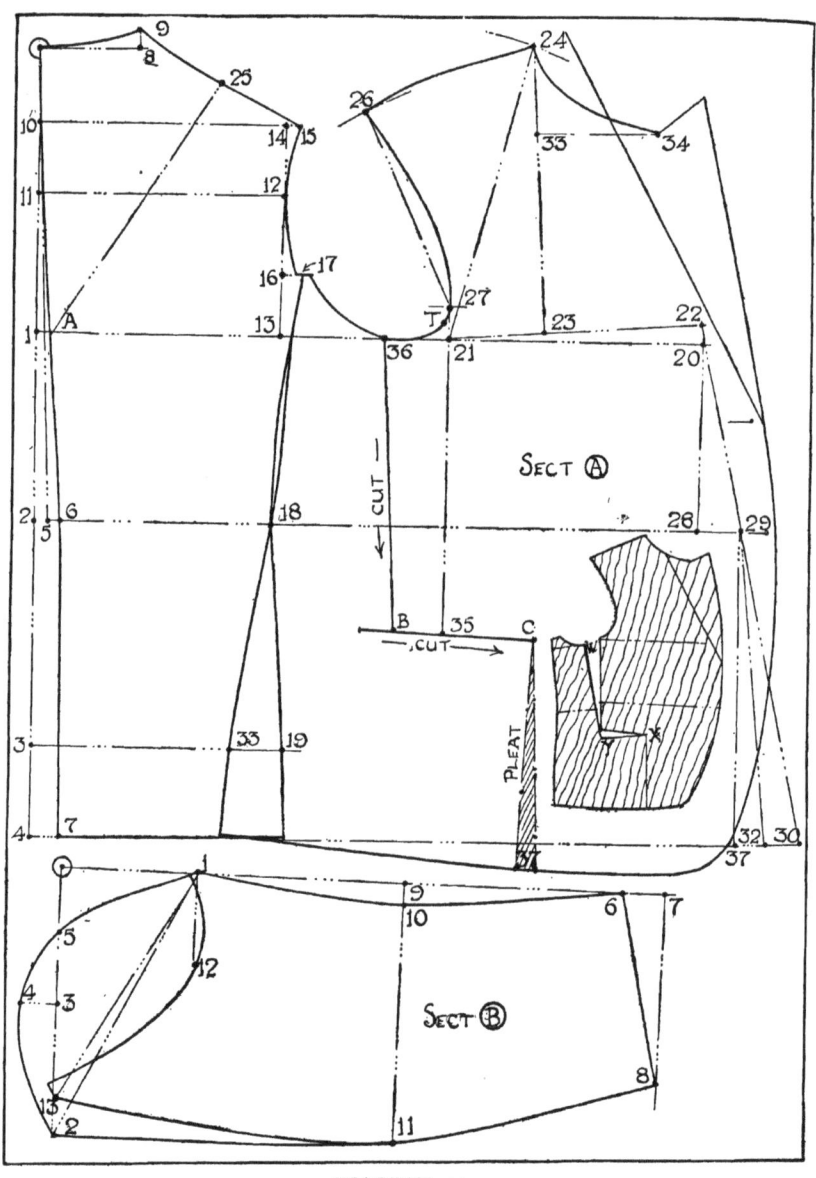

DIAGRAM 23.

CUTTING FOR CORPULENT FIGURES

Join to 6;
8 from 0 = one-sixth scale plus $\frac{1}{4}''$;
9 from 8 = $\frac{3}{4}''$; join to 0;
10 from 1 = one-third over-shoulder measure plus $\frac{3}{4}''$;
11 from 10 = $2\frac{3}{4}''$: square out;
12 from the inside line at 11 = back width plus $\frac{1}{2}''$;
13 and 14 are located by squaring up and down from 12.
15 from 14 = $\frac{1}{2}''$;
Join to 9 for shoulder seam;
16 from 13 = $2\frac{1}{4}''$: square out;
17 from 16 = $\frac{3}{4}''$;
Mark a seam on either side;
18 from 6 = width of back (9) less $1''$;
19 from 3 = 2 to 18 plus $\frac{1}{2}''$;
Shape side seam of back (from 17) as shown;
20 from A = half breast plus $2\frac{1}{2}''$ ($26\frac{1}{2}$);
21 from 20 = across chest ($10\frac{1}{4}$);
22 from 20 = one-eighth disproportion less $\frac{1}{4}''$ ($\frac{3}{4}$): join to 21;
23 from 21 = one-sixth scale;
Square up by line 21–22.
24 from 21 = front shoulder measure less 0 to 8.
Apply the over-shoulder measure less $\frac{1}{2}''$ from A to 25 and then by sweep from 21 to 26.
26 is definitely located by applying the back shoulder width 9 to 15 less $\frac{1}{4}''$ from 24.
27 from 21 = $1''$;
Join to 26 and shape scye as shown.
28 is squared down by breast line from 20.
29 from 28 = $\frac{1}{4}$ disproportion less $\frac{1}{4}''$ ($1\frac{3}{4}$).
Draw through 29 from 22, thus locating 30 on base line.
37 is squared down from 29.
32 is midway between 30 and 31;
Join to 29 for centre line.
Apply half the waist measure plus $2''$ from 6 towards front. In this instance it falls on 29, so there is no waist surplus.
33 from 19 = half the difference between the breast and seat measures plus $\frac{1}{2}''$.
Seeing that there is no waist surplus the side seam of forepart will run through point 18.
33 from 24 = one-sixth scale;
Square out;
34 is on line 33;

Shape neck as shown.
Add $1\frac{1}{2}''$ button stand and complete front.
36 from 21 = $2\frac{1}{2}''$;
35 is $11\frac{1}{2}''$ from 21 for centre of pocket;
Draw a straight line from 36 to rear of pocket centre at B.
Square down from front end of pocket for pleat line 37.
The amount taken out in the pleat at 37 = 37 to 32 less $\frac{1}{4}''$.
Before laying pattern on the cloth cut on line 36 to B, then along pocket mouth to C.
Pleat the bottom over as shown by shaded lines.
The effect of this operation is shown in the shaded inset diagram, which depicts the pattern as it would be laid on the material. The space at W and Y is cut away.
When the cuts at W and Y are sewn up, a receptacle is formed for the prominence of the figure at X.

The Sleeve. Section B

Square lines from 0.
1 from 0 = 12 to 13 of scye;
2 from 1 = 12 to 15 plus 26 to T;
3 is midway between 0 and 2;
4 from 3 = 12 to 15 less $1\frac{1}{4}''$;
5 is midway between 0 and 3;
Shape crown.
6 is the length less back width from 2;
7 from 6 = $1\frac{1}{2}''$;
8 from 6 = one-third scale plus $\frac{1}{2}''$;
9 and 10 are found as before.
11 from 10 = one-third scale plus $2''$;
12 from 1 = half scye width 13 to 21;
13 from T = lower scye (12 round to T).

Notes on the Draft

In the case of a D.B. front, the overlap allowed on the front should follow line 22–29 and 32.
In larger waists the application of the measure on the waist line may go beyond the centre front at 29, thus showing a deficiency. When this occurs, the deficiency must be made up by overlapping the side seam of forepart over back at 18 and not by extending the fronts. Common sense must be used in arranging the back waist suppression at 5 and 6.

CUTTING FOR CORPULENT FIGURES

S.B. VEST BY DIRECT MEASURES. Diagram 24

FEATURES :—*Single-breasted ; no collar ; medium opening.*
MEASURES :—42" *breast ;* 44" *waist ;* 10" *scye depth ;* 17⅝" *waist length ;* 14" *front shoulder ;* 19½" *over shoulder ;* 8½" *across chest ;* 13" *opening ;* 28¾" *full length. Scale* 20". *Disproportion* 6".

INSTRUCTIONS FOR DRAFTING

THE front shoulder is ¼" and the across chest ½" less than the measures as taken for the lounge jacket.

Disproportion and scale quantities are found as described in the lounge draft.

Provision for the figure prominence is arranged by the introduction of a horizontal dart running across the lower end of the pocket.

Dress and D.B. vests are cut on the same lines, the front overlap being based on line 21 to 26.

DRAFT

Square lines from o.
1 from o = scye depth, 10";
2 from o = waist length 17⅝";
3 from 2 = ¼": join to o;
4 from 3 = ¼": curve gradually into the above line as shown;
5 from o = one-sixth scale plus ¼";
6 from 5 = ¾";
Join to o for back neck;
7 from 1 = one-third over-shoulder measure plus ¼": square out;
8 from 7 = one-third scale plus 1¾";
9 is located by squaring down from 8;
10 from A = one-fourth breast plus 1";
11 from A = half breast plus 1½";
12 from 11 = across chest, 8½";
13 from 11 = one-eighth disproportion less ¼";
14 from 12 = one-sixth scale ;
Square upwards by line 12 to 13 ;
15 from 12 = the front shoulder measure less o to 5 ;
Apply the over-shoulder measure less ¼" from A to 16 ; then from 12 to 17 by sweep.
17 is located definitely by applying the back shoulder width (6 to 8) less ¼" from point 15.

18 is 1½" above 12 ;
19 is ¾" from 18 : join to 17 ;
Hollow scye ¼" and curve round to 8 ;
20 is squared down from 11 ;
21 is one-fourth disproportion less ¼" from 20 ;
22 from 15 = one-sixth scale ;
Curve down to 11 ;
23 from 15 = opening measure plus ¼", but less o to 5 ;
24 from 15 = full length plus ¾", but less o to 5 ;
25 is squared down from waist line.
26 is midway between 24 and 25.
Starting at ¾" out from 15, shape the front edge, giving ¾" beyond centre line 11–21–26.
Square down from 10 ;
Curve side seam of forepart slightly as shown.
C from 4 = half waist plus 1½".
In this instance the waist is deficient to the extent shown from 21 to C.
28 from 27 for the side seam of back = 21 to C.
29 from 27 = 2½" for side length.
30 from 29 = two-thirds 20 to 21 and forms the allowance for the pocket vee.

CUTTING FOR CORPULENT FIGURES

The amount taken out of the vee above 27 is $\frac{1}{2}''$ less than 29 to 30. 31 from 28 = 27 to 29 plus $\frac{1}{2}''$.

Notes on the Draft

When difficulty in getting the suit out of the material is experienced, some relief can be obtained by moving the side seam at 10 more towards the front. This increases the back part which is made from lining and correspondingly decreases the cloth space the forepart will take up. Very little stretching is needed in the shoulders.

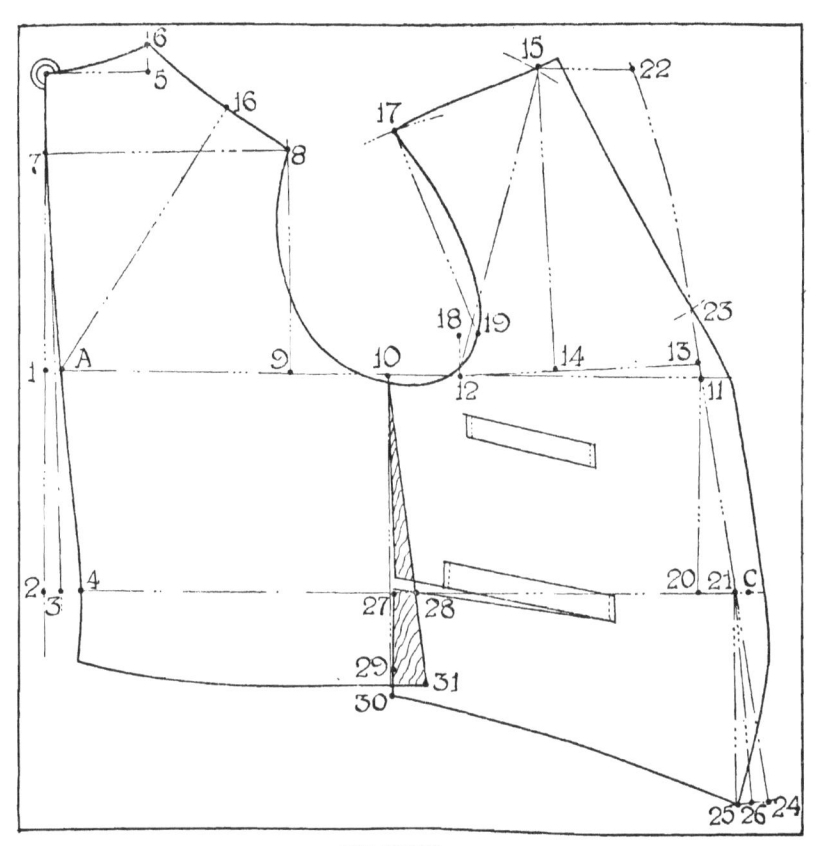

DIAGRAM 24.

MORNING COAT BY PROPORTION. Diagram 25

FEATURES:—*Single-breasted; button two; step collar; high-waisted; cutaway fronts.*

MEASURES:—44″ *breast;* 46″ *waist;* 8½″ *back width;* 18″ *waist length;* 39″ *full length. Scale* 20¾″. *Disproportion* 6″.

INSTRUCTIONS FOR DRAFTING

APART from the treatment at the waist, the construction of this draft is very similar to the ordinary normal draft.

The waist suppression at 15 to 28 to a great extent influences the room over the seat, therefore the standard allowance of ¾″ for spring to the skirt is substituted instead of using the seat measure as in former drafts. Care must be taken in arranging the length of the waist seam of skirt; this must compare with the body part plus a small allowance for fullness that will be introduced at the hip.

DRAFT

Square lines from 0.
1 from 0 = half scale (10⅜);
2 from 0 = waist length (18);
3 from 2 = 1″;
4 from 0 = full length;
Square out from above points.
5 from 2 = 1″: join to 0;
6 from 3 = 1″;
7 from 0 = one-sixth scale plus ¼″;
8 from 7 = ¾″: join to 0;
9 from 0 = one-fourth 0 to 1;
Square out;
10 from 9 = 2¾″: square out;
11 from inside line 10 = back width plus ½″;
12 and 13 are located by squaring from 11;
14 from 13 = ½″: join to 8;
15 from 5 = one-ninth scale plus ¼″;
Connect 11 and 2 and shape blade seam, giving 1″ of round at 16;
Continue from 15 to B.
17 from A = one-third of half breast measure;
18 from 17 = one-fourth of half breast measure, plus 2″;
19 from A = half breast plus 2½″;
20 from 21 = ⅛ disproportion less ¼″: join to 18;
21 from 18 = one-sixth scale;
Square up;
22 from 21 = half scale plus ¼″: join to 14;
23 from 22 = 8 to 14 less ¼″;
24 from 18 = 1″;
Join to 23 and hollow scye ½″;
25 is squared down from the breast line at 19;
26 from 25 = one-fourth disproportion less ¼″ (1¼);
27 from 5 = half waist plus 2″;
28 from 15 = ½″.
NOTE.—The blade suppression 15 to 28 must never be made less than ½″. In this instance the waist surplus shown from 27 to 26 is only ⅛″. Therefore the extra ⅜″ has to be made up by overlapping at the underarm seam 30 to 31.
29 from 12 = 1½″: mark up 1½″ for top of underarm seam.
30 from 28 = 16 to 29 less ½″ for width of side body;
31 from 30 = ⅜″, found as described above.
Sweep B to C by point 11 and square out parallel with waist line from C;
32 from C = 9″;
33 from 32 = ¾″: draw line C to 34;
34 is ½″ below line from 4.
Shape back skirt giving ½″ of round at 35;

CUTTING FOR CORPULENT FIGURES

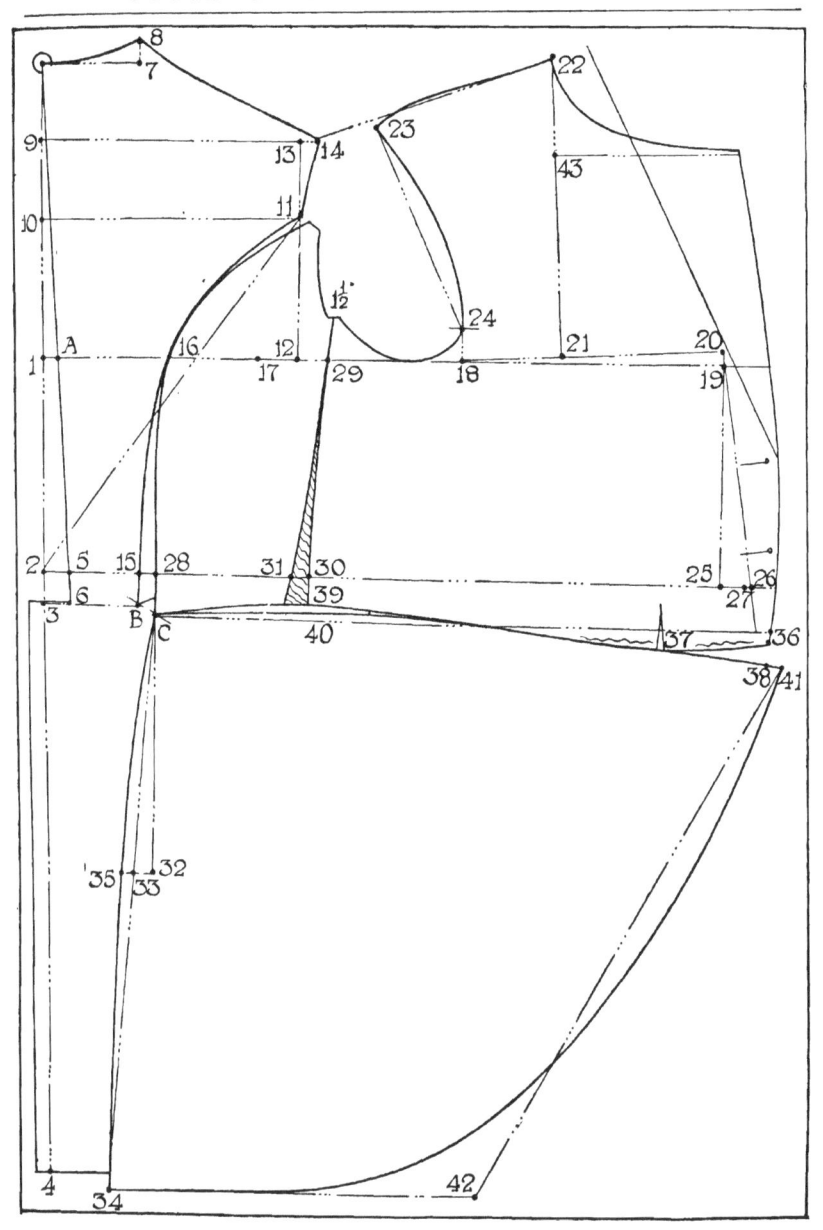

DIAGRAM 25.

CUTTING FOR CORPULENT FIGURES

Allow 1½" button stand at top hole and run off as shown;
36 is ½" below C line;
37 is 1" below C line;
38 from 36 = half 25 to 26.
Shape waist seam of body part to 39, which is ¾" above C line.
Take out ¼" between body part and skirt at 40;
38 to 41 is the amount that the body part has been overlapped at 39;
42 from 34 = half 5 to 26 plus 1";
Join to 41 and use this as a guide line when shaping skirt front.
43 from 22 = one-sixth scale plus ¼";
Square out and shape neck as shown;
The back pleat is finished by marking out 1" from B and squaring down to 4 line.

Notes on the Draft

The waist seam of forepart in the region of 37 should either be drawn in and the resulting fullness pressed upwards over the prominence, or a small vee can be taken out. The amount the waist seam is reduced by this process will enable the skirt to be eased on over the hips.

In a larger waist point 27 may be situated outside of or in front of point 26, thus showing a deficiency. This will not affect the suppression at 28, for the ½" will still have to be taken out. The overlap, however, at 31 will be greater, as it will consist of the amount the waist is short at the front plus the ½" suppression at 28.

CUTTING FOR CORPULENT FIGURES

CHESTERFIELD OVERCOAT. Diagram 26

FEATURES :—*Single-breasted ; step lapel, rolling to $1\frac{1}{2}''$ below breast line ; medium-fitting waist ; centre seam, but no vent.*
MEASURES :—*42" breast ; 44" waist ; 47" seat ; 10" scye depth ; $17\frac{1}{2}''$ waist length ; 42" full length ; $14\frac{5}{8}''$ front shoulder ; $19\frac{1}{2}''$ over shoulder ; $9\frac{3}{8}''$ across chest ; $8\frac{5}{8}''$ across back. Scale 20". Disproportion 6".*

INSTRUCTIONS FOR DRAFTING

THE above measures carry the additions for the overcoat as follows :—Front shoulder plus $\frac{3}{8}''$; back width and across chest plus $\frac{3}{8}''$.

The proportionate method of drafting is the same as prescribed for the ordinary Chesterfield. Disproportion is found as for other garments.

For sac coats the disproportion only affects the fronts, the sides remaining the same.

THE DRAFT

Square lines from 0.
1 from 0 = scye depth 10" ;
2 from 0 = waist length plus $\frac{1}{4}''$;
3 from 2 = 1 to 2 plus $1\frac{1}{2}''$;
4 from 0 = full length ;
Square out from the above points ;
5 from 2 = $\frac{1}{2}''$;
Join to 0 ;
6 from 5 = $\frac{1}{2}''$;
Curve gradually into the above line ;
7 from 4 = 2 to 6 ;
Connect to 6 ;
8 from 1 = one-third over-shoulder measure plus $\frac{3}{4}''$: square out ;
9 from 8 = $2\frac{1}{4}''$;
10 from 0 = one-sixth scale plus $\frac{1}{4}''$;
11 from 10 = $\frac{3}{4}''$: join to 0 ;
12 from 9 = back width plus $\frac{1}{2}''$ ($9\frac{1}{8}$) ;
13 and 14 are located by squaring from 12 ;
15 from 14 = $\frac{1}{2}''$: join to 11 ;
16 from 13 = $1\frac{1}{4}''$;
17 from 16 = $\frac{3}{4}''$:
Mark a seam on either side.
18 from 6 = the net back width less $\frac{1}{4}''$;
19 from 3 = 2 to 18 plus $\frac{1}{4}''$;
Shape side seam of back as shown.
20 from A = half breast plus $3\frac{3}{4}''$;

21 from 20 = across chest $9\frac{3}{8}''$;
22 from 21 = $\frac{1}{8}$ disproportion less $\frac{1}{4}''$: join to 21 ;
23 from 21 = one-sixth scale plus $\frac{1}{4}''$;
Square up by line 21 to 23 ;
24 from 21 by sweep = the front shoulder measure less back neck 0 to 10 ;
Apply the over-shoulder measure less $\frac{1}{4}''$ from A to 25 ; then by sweep from 21 to 26 ;
26 is located definitely by applying the back shoulder width 11 to 15 less $\frac{1}{4}''$ from 24 ;
Mark up $\frac{1}{4}''$ from 21 and join to 26 : hollow scye $\frac{1}{2}''$;
27 from 21 = $\frac{3}{4}''$ for scye base.
28 is squared from 20 on breast line ;
29 from 28 = $\frac{1}{4}$ disproportion less $\frac{1}{4}''$;
Apply waist measure plus $3\frac{3}{4}''$ from 6 towards front. In this instance it falls on point 29, therefore there is nothing to take out nor anything to be overlapped at the side seam at 18.
30 from 19 = half difference between breast and seat measures plus $\frac{1}{4}''$: draw side seam from 17 through 18 and 30 ;
Draw through 29 from 20 extending 9" down to 31.

CUTTING FOR CORPULENT FIGURES

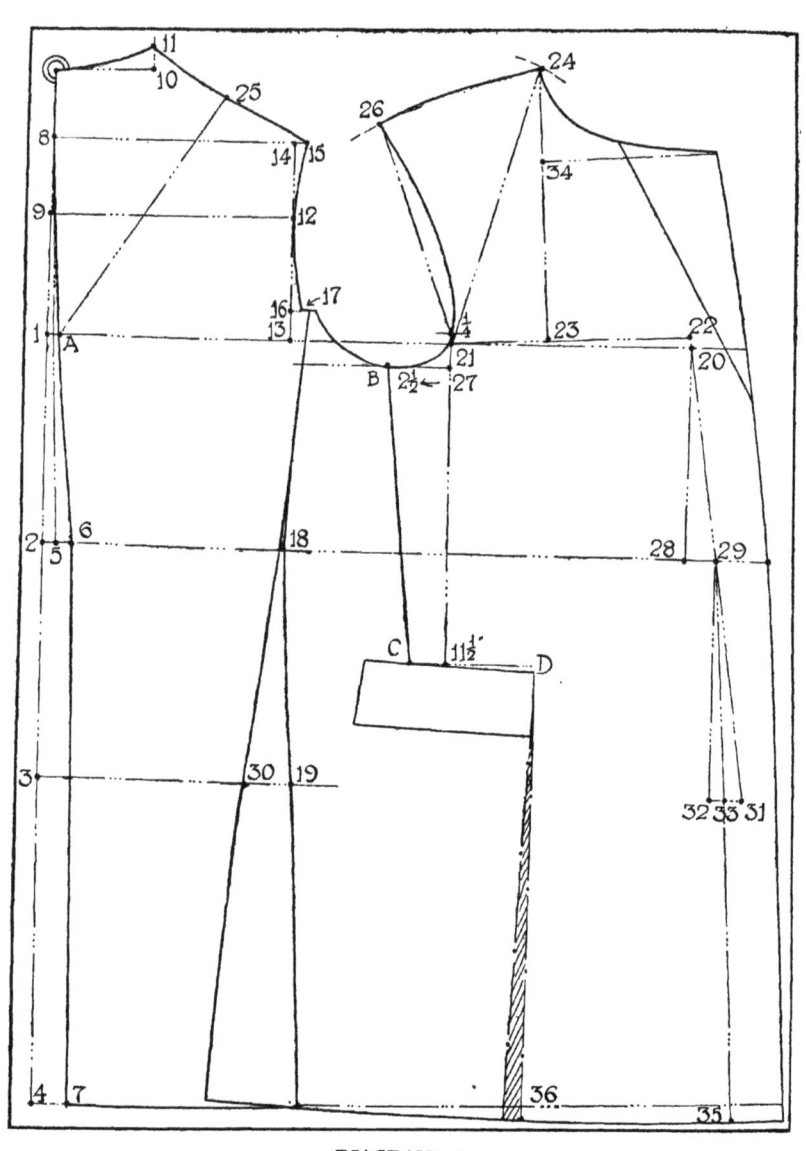

DIAGRAM 26.

CUTTING FOR CORPULENT FIGURES

32 is squared from 29;
33 is midway between 32 and 31;
Draw through 33 from 29 for actual centre front line;
Give 2" overlap beyond centre line;
34 from 24 = one-sixth scale plus ¼";
Shape lapel and neck on to this line;
Give ¾" below bottom construction line and complete outline.
Mark down 11½" from 21 for centre pocket.
Run the underarm seam from a point 2½" back from 27 to rear of pocket.
Square down from front end of pocket at D and mark a pleat at 36. The amount taken out in the pleat is equal to 32 to 33.

The pattern is arranged on lines described for the lounge. The seam from B to C and the pocket mouth from C to D are cut before the pleat is taken out at 36.

NOTES ON THE DRAFT

Where a looser fitting but still slightly shaped waist is desired, a little more overlap can be given at the waist 18 and seat 30.

If a double-breasted front is required, 4" to 4½" is added beyond centre line, care being taken to follow line 29 to 33 below the waist.

The sleeve is the same as for the ordinary Chesterfield.

GENTLEMEN'S GARMENT CUTTING

By PERCIVAL THICKETT

(*Author of "Defects and Remedies," "Body Coats," etc.*)

VARIATIONS FROM THE NORMAL DRAFT

Diagram 27

THE accompanying page of diagrams illustrates how the normal pattern will have to be adjusted to meet the requirements of irregular figures. It is assumed that the original block has been constructed on a proportionate basis and is one that will provide a satisfactory fit for the normal type of figure. When making the adjustments it is advisable to work on a low estimate and not make the alteration from the block too pronounced.

Especially is this precaution necessary when one is working from descriptions provided by travellers or agents.

It is possible to have a combination of the examples shown here, such as a " stooping figure with square shoulders," or a " short stocky figure that is very erect."

When this occurs, it is better to make the adjustment for size before that for attitude.

If Direct Measures are taken, most of the changes will be automatically embodied in the process of drafting. In the diagrams shown, the normal block is outlined by solid lines and the deviations by dash or dot and dash lines.

SECTION A. LONG NECK OR SLOPING SHOULDERS

The alteration for this figure is shown by dash lines.

Vertical lines are drawn through back and front neck points, and the extra height added to accord with the figure as shown from 1 to 2 and 3 to 4.

Connect 4 and 5; also 2 and 6.

Raise the neck back at 7 to agree with the quantity raised at 4.

SECTION A. SHORT NECK OR SQUARE SHOULDERS

The alteration for this figure is shown by dot and dash lines and is executed in the reverse way described for the long neck figure.

VARIATIONS FROM NORMAL DRAFT

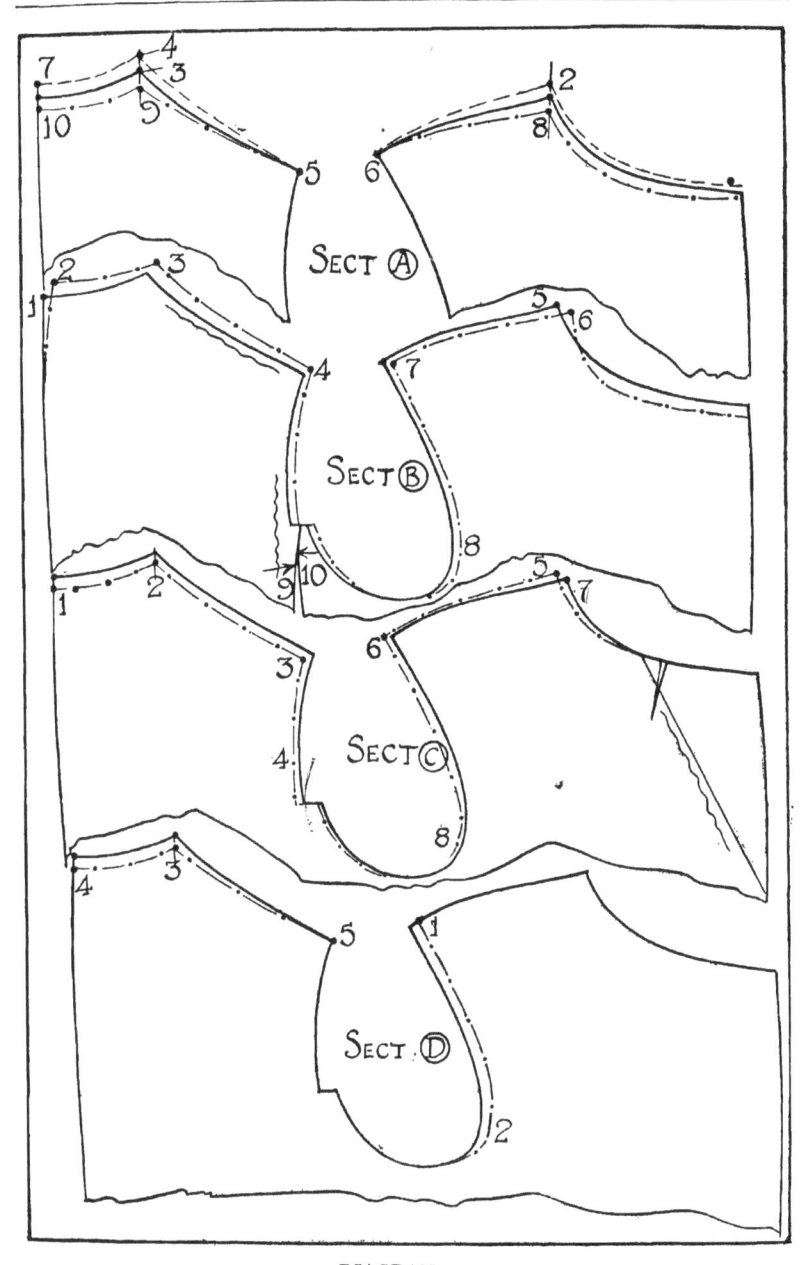

DIAGRAM 27.

VARIATIONS FROM NORMAL DRAFT

Lower the front from 1 to 8 and the back from 3 to 9.

Lower centre at 10 to agree with the drop at 9.

Section B. Stooping Figure

Raise the back from 1 to 2 and bring in point 2 half the quantity raised to give the necessary round over the blade. Point 3 is raised and advanced to agree with the position of 2.

Raise point 4, and if the figure requires a wider back extend down the back scye as shown.

Drop the front the same amount the back has been raised and carry it forward a corresponding amount.

Drop shoulder end at 7 and hollow scye at 8.

Full on the shoulder of back and shrink the back scye in the region of wavy lines.

If the coat has been cut out, the backs can be passed up to obtain the necessary length. To do this balance marks are placed at the side seams as shown at 9 and 10. These go together when sewing the side seam.

Section C. Erect Figure

Shorten the back right across as shown at 1, 2, and 3 and narrow the back scye at 4.

Raise the front shoulder seam right across as shown at 5 and 6.

Crooken the shoulder by receding the neck point from 7 to 5.

Widen the across chest at 8 and take out a small vee in the neck and through the crease line as shown.

Section D. Short Stocky Figure

This particular type is generally blessed with a very large upper arm section. Other features are: a narrow shoulder and very upright carriage.

Advance the scye, say $\frac{1}{2}''$, from the shoulder seam (1 to 2).

Lower the back at 3 and 4 and run out to the shoulder end at 5 as set down for square shoulders.